CHASE AMANTE

HOW TO TEXT A GIRL

A GIRLS CHASE GUIDE

Girls Chase Books
www.girlschase.com

First Girls Chase international mass market paperback edition, December 2016

The Girls Chase name and logo are trademarks of Girls Chase, Inc.

The publisher is not responsible for websites (or their content) that are not owned by the publisher.

Library of Congress Cataloging-in-Publication Data

Amante, Chase.
How to Text a Girl / Chase Amante.
ISBN: 978-0-9833904-2-8

Contents

Introduction

This book is not about getting you more texts from girls. If it was about that, I would've titled it *How to Have Long Text Conversations with a Girl*.

It's not about that, because I don't think that's what you actually want. I don't think you actually want to be as clever as you can be in your texting. And I don't think you actually want to make her fall in love with your texts.

I think what you actually want is to be able to get her to say YES when you ask her to meet up. So that's what this book is about.

Throughout this book, I'm going to challenge some of the most cherished conventional notions of "good texting." If some of these challenges I toss your way make you a little uncomfortable, that's good. What I want you to do when that happens is to take the empiricist's mindset and say "Okay, let me try it out."

Take it for a spin and see what happens.

Your intuition might say "She would *never* go for that," but sometimes your intuition lies. Especially when it comes to doing something new – or in a way you haven't done before.

The focus here is not to build up your ego or fill your head with platitudes. Instead, the sole goal of this book – and the only thing I care about – is to get her off the phone and on a date with you.

In case this is the first time we've met, my name's Chase Amante. I'm quite possibly the world's foremost expert on dating. At the very least, I run the world's most popular website on the subject (that's GirlsChase.com, with half a million unique visitors each month), where I've written 5 million words in the last 3 years alone. My specialty – my angle – is that I teach you how to get girls to chase YOU. Sound absurd? It isn't. In fact, throughout this book you'll see **words in bold**[1] accompanied by footnotes pointing you to articles found on the site. Check those articles out and your eyes will begin to open. Now, since you can't just tap on the words and be taken straight to the articles like you can in the digital version of this book, you'll need to visit GirlsChase.com and use the search function to look up the articles by their title. I promise it'll be worth the effort!

I know you've seen the guys who just sit back and have girls hound them to meet up. And fortunately, it's not just looks that get girls to chase. I sat down to figure out the dating game and I discovered the question that drove my passion: How do I get girls to chase me?

I approached thousands of women. I went on hundreds of dates. I whisked girls off to bed, and I took some of them as girlfriends. And I got good.

---

[1] Article titles will be found in the footnotes. You can visit girlschase.com and use the search bar to look up the article by title, or you can find the full URLs in Appendix B.

One night, having already taught a fair few students of seduction at this point, I found myself with a buddy. He told me about this girl he was trying to get to come meet him. But she just wouldn't come out.

So I asked him for some detail on the situation: how he knew her, what their history was, what he'd tried already.

And then I asked to see his phone.

The next thing I did was write a simple, tight little text. I passed the phone back to him to read over and send if he approved. He did, and hit *send*.

Two minutes later, she responded saying she had to be up at 7 AM the next day and had to get to bed. It was already 11 PM.

But then she added, "But okay, I can come out for drinks tonight."

This floored my friend. And while I'd known I could do it for myself, it was actually the first time I'd sat down to author a text for someone else.

See, my skill at texting kind of crept up on me. When I first started meeting girls, I could sometimes get flakey girls to do a 180 and meet up. Even then, I had some intuition; what I didn't have yet was a method.

More often than not, I'd get stuck with go-nowhere numbers no matter what I texted.

I never set out to learn to text the way I had set out to learn conversation or physical escalation. It just happened organically as an outgrowth of my desire to excel with girls (plus the sheer volume of phone numbers I tore through).

I went with my friend on the date, because I was going to help him recognize when to take her home, too. She was already excited by the time she met us at the bar.

Oftentimes, that's the effect of just one great text:

It energizes her to meet you.

The girl ended up agreeing to go home with my friend. She bailed at the last minute (literally; she stopped the cab 20 feet from his apartment and got out). But she would've been his had he been a little warmer and a little more persistent. What's important here is, he got her out to meet him – he got a chance – because of a single text.

Once I realized the power my texting held, I began to take on texting students. And soon thereafter, my texting was getting guys dates, lays, and girlfriends.

A girl who'd stopped texting a guy – I'd give him a text, and she'd text back immediately and ask him to meet.

Boom!

A girl saying she had a boyfriend and was sorry she couldn't meet – I'd tell the guy what to text her, and she'd schedule a date the next day. They'd have sex, and the boyfriend (if he even existed) wouldn't even come up.

Bam!

A guy with a booty call who wanted something more serious – I'd give him a few words, and she'd be over at his place that night, doing some decidedly non-serious things to him.

Kapow!

And I of course incorporated these techniques myself, even on girls who weren't that sold on me at first. A confident, brief, and snappy texter is rare enough that girls will meet you on curiosity alone. And if they're curious enough to meet you, they're curious enough to date and sleep with you.

Throughout these texting adventures, my students and I discussed and documented what worked, what didn't, the hows and whys as we perceived them, and the tricks and traps. What follows in this book is a set of instructions on how to achieve the same results with texting that my students and I have. It adapts some popular articles I've written for GirlsChase.com over the years. It also includes some new content never before published elsewhere.

Once you get texting down, getting quality dates becomes almost too easy. Being able to quickly turn her contact info into a meet-up is a game changer. It gives you so many more opportunities to succeed with women.

If you're ready to use the text message to achieve incredible results with girls, you'll love this book.

1

The Four Kinds of Texters

"The medium is the message." So said Marshall McLuhan in *Understanding Media: The Extensions of Man* (McLuhan, 1994). McLuhan argued, just as the digital age was dawning, that not only do we adapt our communication style to the channels we use... but that any channel we choose to use itself tells the person we're talking to what kind of message it is.

Texting works best if you think of it as a quick, efficient way to ping girls, make simple connections, and arrange the logistics for dates. You can use it for updates ("There in 5 minutes") or to ask questions ("Grab a table yet?").

Yet, if you try using it like a text version of how you'd talk to her in person or on a phone or video call, you'll face a lot of unnecessary hurdles.

To begin our book, I want to introduce you to four kinds of texters. Three of these texters don't fully respect the medium (texting) as a message (quick, simple, and logistical). The fourth one does – and he gets the best results. Much of this book will be about why, and the rest of it will be about how to text girls like he does.

Before we get to that kind of texter, first I want to tell you about the three far more common forms of texters on the dating market. These I've affectionately dubbed Clueless Boring Questions Guy™, Endless Conversations Guy™, and Really, Incredibly Witty and Interesting Guy™.

The Three Normal Guy Texting Styles

There are three strains of text messaging styles prevalent among the men out there today:

1. Clueless Boring Questions Guy™
2. Endless Conversations Guy™
3. Really, Incredibly Witty and Interesting Guy™

I've ranked these strains in order of prevalence, from most to least encountered. Yet even though he's last, the Really, Incredibly Witty and Interesting Guy™ is not all that uncommon.

Before we dive into what to do with girls to actually get results out of texting, let's start with a look at what these three guys do, and why it doesn't work. Try not to be miffed if you realize you're one of these guys halfway in... because if you are, you're exactly the target demographic of this book. There's hope.

Can't fix the problem unless you know the problem exists in the first place, right?

Clueless Boring Questions Guy™

To women, the most diabolically annoying texter is the Clueless Boring Questions Guy™, hereafter abbreviated as CBQG. CBQG has zero clue how to text girls, what girls would like to see in a text message, or even what girls are like most of the time in general, period. At no time has CBQG ever sat down and asked himself:

"If **I** was a girl, how would **I** respond to a message like this?"

He immediately assumes that all women are like him – lonely and without many options. Thus, they should be thrilled to get texts from him, even if they're all just clueless boring questions like:

"What's up?"
"How's it going?"
"How was your weekend?"
"What are you doing?"
"Do you have plans?"

CBQG assumes that girls must love getting texts like this from him. After all, he'd love getting texts like this from girls. So of course it must go both ways.

CBQG often becomes frustrated when girls don't answer his questions. He wonders why he doesn't get replies. He thinks girls are difficult to understand and make things needlessly complicated.

He never stops to realize she isn't there in person and doesn't get the same level of context and expressiveness from him she would if he was there (Critchley, Rotshtein, Nagai, O'Doherty, Mathias, & Dolan, 2005).

At no point does CBQG sit down and think to himself: "Lame guys inundate most girls all day with lame requests. Most guys text, write, and say to girls the same lame things all the time. Oh no! If I send girls lame texts, they'll assume I'm lame, too!"

This never occurs to him, because CBQG knows himself so well that he knows that he's not lame. He assumes that everyone else must know this, too... even if he behaves the same way that other men, who actually are lame, do.

"She'll know I'm not lame, even if I seem totally lame," CBQG thinks. "Otherwise, she's totally shallow and not worth my time!"

CBQG believes that it's women's responsibility to recognize his inner awesomeness. Girls must fight through the lameness he exhibits on the outside to discover his awesomeness inside.

CBQG spends many nights alone, angry, hurt, and confused by how the world can be so confusing and so cold.

Endless Conversations Guy™

Endless Conversations Guy™, hereafter ECG, is usually a CBQG who cleaned up his act. One day he looked at his phone, which was devoid of replies to the texts he'd sent out, and said to himself:

"If **I** was a girl, how would **I** respond to a message like this?"

...and in a flash of sudden insight, he realized he'd been doing it all wrong.

ECG is, you might say, on a more enlightened plane than CBQG. He's realized the need to engage a girl in dialogue. And he's realized girls don't want to answer clueless boring questions.

Unfortunately, ECG still doesn't get much further beyond "engage her in dialogue" – and there he's usually stuck. ECG's conversations tend to look something like this:

> **ECG:** Hey Shirley, how'd your weekend go? I saw some friends Saturday, but yesterday was all just relaxing.
>
> **Girl:** Hey, it was all right. My friend from out of town came to visit, so we went to a couple of restaurants and saw some sights... that was about it.
>
> **ECG:** Cool, what sights did you see?
>
> **Girl:** Oh, you know, Sea World, the harbor, just the usual things.
>
> **ECG:** You know, I've been living here for 5 years and I've never seen Sea World. Everyone keeps telling me I should go.
>
> **Girl:** I know, I didn't go to Sea World until I was 19, and I grew up here. Isn't that ridiculous? But you SHOULD go, it's a lot of fun.
>
> **ECG:** When I used to live on the East Coast, sometimes we'd go down and visit the Baltimore Aquarium. I don't know if Sea World's like an aquarium at all, but that place was amazing. I kind of miss going now.

Girl: It's not really an aquarium... more like a place with sea animals that does shows.

ECG: Yeah, they had some of those at the Baltimore Aquarium too.

Girl: Cool.

ECG: Hey, so [conversation continues]

ECG treats his texting like written phone conversations. He doesn't recognize texting is supposed to be simpler in both language and function (Holtgraves & Paul, 2013). He doesn't know that the more time she spends with him in text chats and the less time she spends with him in person, the worse she feels about him, as researchers found studying teenage couples in 2014 (Luo, 2014). He never realizes these endless conversations are actually boring, pointless, and inane. He doesn't realize most girls who engage in these with him are either (a) just doing it because they're also bored, or (b) just too nice to not send back a response. To him, it feels like he has unlocked the key to texting girls: just keep texting.

As far as ECG knows, this is just another normal conversation... in which he imagines he is inching his way ever closer to becoming this girl's beau... every sent text bringing him another couple centimeters nearer her heart....

You can imagine how frustrated he gets when a girl he has spent so much time with in endless conversations... endlessly dodges his date requests – and how perplexed he is to discover, after weeks or months of conversations, that some other guy has managed to become her boyfriend.

"How can this be?" ECG thinks. "I thought we had such special conversations!"

He's bewildered... it just doesn't make sense. Why would she spend SO much time talking to him and then go date someone else?

Really, Incredibly Witty and Interesting Guy™

Last but not least is Really, Incredibly Witty and Interesting Guy™, henceforth RIWIG. RIWIG is the next stage of evolution after ECG. He's a man who has realized that endless conversations don't work. They're boring, kill his intrigue, and every guy and his brother engage in them fruitlessly.

RIWIG has more experience with girls than either CBQG or ECG. He knows women react well to humor and prefer interesting **bad boys**[2] to uninteresting **nice guys**[3].

"So," goes RIWIG's line of thinking, "what could be better than being a bad boy via text message?"

Most texting advice you'll see online or hear from friends comes from RIWIGs. They've cracked the texting code, they'll tell you. They've figured out how to create the emotions they want in women... desire, laughter, intrigue. Being really, incredibly witty and interesting over text is the way to get girls attracted to you.

And to be fair, RIWIG is far more interesting and captivating than either CBQG or ECG. It's not even close. RIWIG leaves those guys in his dust. Just as CBQG can't hold a candle to ECG, ECG's

---

[2] GirlsChase.com — "Why Girls Like Bad Boys"
[3] GirlsChase.com — "Why Nice Guys Finish Last"

odds to beat RIWIG in a text fight are about as good as a medieval pikeman's odds against a Navy SEAL with a minigun and a grenade launcher.

RIWIG's text conversations tend to go something like this:

> **RIWIG:** Oh man, I just had WAY too much food. Never should've eaten that last drumstick. Advice: gluttony doesn't just make you fat, it's also REALLY uncomfortable.

> **Girl:** lol where were you and why'd you eat so much?

> **RIWIG:** Friend had a birthday party. There was far too much to eat; I felt a moral obligation to ensure there weren't unnecessary leftovers.

> **Girl:** Did you save any for me?

> **RIWIG:** Thought about it; decided against it. You should be grateful I prevented you from enduring a similar fate to mine.

> **Girl:** But I want some too!

> **RIWIG:** You know what, miss... you are coming on WAY too strong right now. Most women are a lot more... CIRCUMSPECT... when they say things like that to me.

> **Girl:** I'm talking about the food, DUH!

> **RIWIG:** That's what they always say...

> **Girl:** You are such a dork.

> **RIWIG:** Hey, so [conversation continues]

I was this guy for a long time. And it's obviously a big step up from ECG. But even with his really, incredibly witty and interesting text banter, RIWIG has the following problems: (a) women will still often be dodgy about setting up dates, and (b) when the dates ARE set up, the girl often treats RIWIG as a **boyfriend candidate**[4] (i.e., she puts up obstacles to sex).

"What gives?" RIWIG thinks. "I was interesting, witty, sexy... everything a woman looks for in a lover, NOT a boyfriend! And she's STILL treating me like a potential boyfriend! Clearly I need to be even MORE witty and interesting."

But being wittier and more interesting isn't the answer. In fact, the answer is something much simpler than CBQG, ECG, or RIWIG think it could ever be.

The Fourth Kind of Texter

There's good news for our heroes Clueless Boring Questions Guy™, Endless Conversations Guy™, and Really, Incredibly Witty and Interesting Guy™. The good news is there's a fourth texter with a style they haven't tried out, thought up, or looked into yet.

And he doesn't need clueless boring questions. He doesn't require endless conversations. Heck, he doesn't even need to be all that witty or interesting. All you've got to do to use his style is be able to send simple text messages... and tell the girl you want a date with her BEFORE you get her phone number.

---

[4] GirlsChase.com – "Does She Want You as a Boyfriend... or Something Else?"

If we had to give this kind of texter a name, I think it'd be Just Gets It Guy™ (JGIG). His style is all about keeping things simple and to-the-point. The truth is, less "natural" media (like email and text messaging) are less satisfying for people to deal with (Kock, 2004). You want to spend as *little* time with her in less natural media as possible – and as much time as possible with her in person.

I adopted the JGIG style only after I reached a point where I didn't have time to engage in long text conversations. I didn't have time to think up incredibly witty, interesting things to say. And at that point, even when I *did* have the time, I didn't care to do all that work anymore.

What I found was, this new style was far more effective.

I started to teach friends how to text girls with this simplistic model of texting. All of a sudden, they were lining up as many dates as they could handle. I've since taught this method to thousands of students at Girls Chase.

But a lot of guys still don't really get it. They're still trying to mix in CBQG or ECG or RIWIG elements with this style of texting. It's like taking a gourmet recipe and throwing in extra eggs and baking soda because those ingredients work great in other things you make. The end result is not something better. It's something worse.

That's why I put together this book: to provide a more in-depth, more meaty, and more behind-the-scenes psychological approach that helps you fully understand: (a) what girls are thinking, (b) why they react the way they do, and (c) what it is that those other texting styles just don't take into account.

You'll get plenty of examples of how the Just Gets It Guy™ texts girls in this book. In fact, unless I tell you otherwise, every example you see from here on out is one of his.

In Summary...

In this chapter, we covered the four kinds of texters:

1. Clueless Boring Questions Guy™
2. Endless Conversations Guy™
3. Really, Incredibly Witty and Interesting Guy™
4. Just Gets It Guy™

We discussed the problems each of the first three texters run into, and why they run into them. We looked at the mindsets behind their texting strategies, and we gave you a taste of what *good* texting – in the form of Just Gets It Guy™ – looks and feels like.

Next up, I'll introduce you to the eight "ground rules" of texting: mental foundations that are crucial to get you thinking about text conversations the right way.

After that, I'll arm you with a simple structure to follow to get girls out on dates. Then we'll open up the hood and look deep into "text tech": little things you can do with texts that work to up your odds.

2

Ground Rules of Texting

Text Messaging ABCs

Our first order of business is to deprogram you from bad texting mentalities, ineffective approaches, and misconceptions. These are the things that make texting harder than it needs to be, causing men to send texts that just don't work.

To do this, I'm going to give you the eight "mental foundations" of texting you need to have going in. These foundations let you think about texting a girl in an effective way that gets her excited to see you and ready to come out on a date.

#1: Faulty Models Are Your Responsibility to Fix, Not Women's

One of the themes **I stress**[5] is this: you can blame OTHER people for YOUR life, or you can go out and get what you want. You absolutely can't do both, however.

It's blame and be miserable, or accept responsibility and go get what you want.

As you go down the texting styles, you'll find the less evolved a man's style is, the more he blames girls. Clueless Boring Questions Guy™ is the worst... to him, nothing is his fault.

The worse a man is with women, the more fault he perceives in women.

What's the reason for this phenomenon?

It's a symptom of faulty mental models.

Women trade phone numbers a lot. And they don't like getting clueless boring questions from anyone... even close friends, family, lovers, boyfriends, etc.

So just imagine how a girl feels when she gets questions like this from some guy she doesn't know all that well, or some guy she met in passing at work or at the bar or on the street or in class, even if he attracted her (at first).

That's right: she pigeonholes him as someone who's a liability and not a joy to be around. Her interest in him goes from whatever it was before the clueless boring questions started, straight to zero.

---

[5] GirlsChase.com – "How Victim Mentality Can Stifle Your Life – and Luck with Women"

It's not girls who are the problem. It's the model you've got.

If girls don't think, act, or respond the way you think they should, it doesn't mean all 3.5 billion human females need to change. What it means is that your mental model must change to accommodate the way women actually are.

This chapter is about changing that model you've got.

#2: Phone Numbers are Easy

One of the reasons inexperienced guys struggle so much with the idea of texting needing to be ironed out is because they view phone numbers as a BIG DEAL!

The problem is that, to girls, phone numbers are NOT a big deal!

An inexperienced guy gets a girl's phone number, and it feels like a colossal achievement. Now he can rest. For all intents and purposes, he's got a girlfriend.

Except she doesn't see it that way. For girls, a phone number is just the START. And girls give their numbers out all the time to guys whom they never end up talking to or seeing ever again.

You're not the only one asking her. Other guys ask her, too. And she says yes to some of them, sometimes.

Phone numbers mean NOTHING. They're a dime a dozen... nothing more than a chance. They are NOT a guarantee, a promise, or an assurance of any kind. "Here's my phone number" does not equal "Sure, we can have sex." It doesn't equal "Would you like to be my boyfriend?" nor does it even mean "I'm definitely going to talk to you again!"

If it helps, you can think of a phone number simply as "Here's a way you can get me to meet you again if you do a good job making me want to."

Once you start seeing numbers this way, you'll instantly begin to realize why clueless boring questions are a death sentence. That is, it's far easier to say "no" to you over the phone than in real life.

And if you're just going to be boring and clueless on the phone, what's she supposed to do... be excited?

Phone numbers are not a promise; they are an opportunity.

#3: Emotions Don't "Stick"

When you first trade numbers with a girl, you might leave on cloud nine, dreaming about the amazing future you'll have with her. Maybe you had an amazing interaction with her and really **connected with her**[6] on a pretty deep level. Chances are she's forgotten all about you.

Oh sure, she might still be thinking about you. But you don't know that, and it's much better to assume that she isn't. If she isn't, how's she going to react to your first text?

Pretend she's forgotten EVERYTHING about you... because it's more likely she's rushed, put-upon, angry, and annoyed from other things in her life.

Is your text going to make her smile? Is it going to take a load off her shoulders? Or is it just something else to make her feel even

---

[6] GirlsChase.com — "Get to Know a Girl: Connection-Building Tactics"

MORE rushed, put-upon, angry, and annoyed? If you're not sure, ask yourself this:

If I was really rushed, put-upon, angry, and annoyed right now... and I received this text message randomly from someone I could hardly remember... what would my emotion be?

If the answer is "even more rushed, put-upon, angry, and annoyed," head back to the drawing board. Find something that better evokes the right emotions.

If she remembers you, great – that's a bonus. You'll still send her a great text message, and she'll be even HAPPIER to hear from you. But if she doesn't... if she's forgotten all about you... and you send her the right message... you still stand a good chance of getting her out anyway.

#4: People Want You to Reduce Their Cognitive Loads (Not Pile On)

Imagine you are SUPER busy. You're stressed like crazy, running around trying to get a million things done that you HAVE to get done. You want to scream and punch the wall and pull your hair out you're so far behind on things.

Then, you get a random text message from some guy you met at a bar the other day who seemed like kind of an okay guy.

"What's up?" it says.

What's up? you think to yourself, angry and annoyed. *What's up??!! What, am I supposed to sit here and figure out what that means?*

Like, you just want to shoot the shit, like I have time for that? Or, you want to ask me for some kind of favor, or want me to offer something to you? I don't have the patience for this!

This is the thought process of even a moderately busy girl when she gets a message like this. In 2005, Ned Kock, Chair of the Department of MIS and Decision Science at Texas A&M, showed that as people use less natural media (like texting), the amount of thinking they have to do shoots up – that is to say, their cognitive costs increase (Kock, 2005). With no context to frame the message, ambiguous messages like "What's up?" are some of the most mentally taxing messages of all. And that makes them among the least likely to get a response.

Personally, I won't respond to these messages when I get them from GIRLS. And I'm a GUY. Most guys WANT to get messages like this from girls. Girls do NOT want to get messages like this from guys, because these messages raise mental loads.

The second a girl reads a message like this, her mind puts everything else on hold to ask itself: "Who is this? What does he want? Is he going to ask me for something? Should I respond? How should I respond? Should I tell him about my day? Should I tell him how stressed I am? Is he going to start sending me lots of messages if I reply? Is he waiting for me to take the lead here? Is he going to ask me out? Does he expect ME to ask HIM out?"

Much of the time, her mind will just decide this is too many questions to answer, and it'll worry about this later. She closes her phone, never to reply.

None of this is because she's mean or cold or rude or aloof or even disinterested. It's just too much thinking to do, so she puts it off... and then forgets about it. Or she remembers it again later... only to put it off even further.

Like it or not, when it comes to less-clear media like text messaging, the burden of making the meaning of a message clear falls on the person sending the message, not the one receiving it (Kock, 2007). It's on you to make it clear what you mean – she isn't going to sit there and try to figure it out.

You must strive to be crystal clear and easy to respond to in your messages. It's vital you reduce mental loads as much as possible.

Don't make her think. Don't make her wonder. Don't get her into giant open loops she needs to spend huge amounts of mental processing power on. That's an invitation to ignore you.

And you don't want her to see you as inconsiderate or socially stunted, either. **Socially savvy people**[7] don't shift big mental loads onto people via text. They make things easy. They take loads off. You should, too.

That means, instead of "What's up?" you can say:

> Hey Charlene, hope you had a kick ass weekend. Mine was solid and restful... just what I needed. When's good for you to grab that bite this week? Let me know when your schedule's clear, and let's set it up.

No wondering what your motives are. No asking herself what you're after. No deliberating on how to respond, or even if she should respond at all. All she's got to do is tell you when her schedule's open.

---

[7] GirlsChase.com – "Ultimate Social Calibration: Stop Climbing the Social Ladder"

It's easy.

And because it's easy, you're orders of magnitude more likely to get what you want: a date.

#5: You Must Keep Your Eye on the Ball

Quick, how many great relationships in your life stemmed from long text conversations? How many friendships? Girlfriends?

If you're like most people, the answer is this: **0**.

That's because texting is an atrocious way to build meaningful relationships. This is not how to text girls at all.

Guys still keep doing it though. They do it in droves. And the reason why is because their eyes are not on the ball.

If you've ever found yourself mired in long text message conversations, I bet you've never stopped to ask: "Where is this going?" And if you did, I'm certain your answer to yourself would be "I have NO idea!"

That is not how to run a texting conversation.

It's not how to run anything.

Imagine if a sailor set out on a ship into the great blue sea with no idea where he was going. "I'm going to find a beautiful, uninhabited island out there with a pirate's buried treasure and I'm going to get rich!" he told himself. "I just have to sail around enough until I find it!" Now, after he sets off on his voyage, he might end up finding that one island in the vast ocean with a few doubloons buried in a chest. But it's far more likely he'll die at sea or return to port, frustrated and bitter.

When you shoot in the dark, you almost always miss the mark.

With very few exceptions, texting is terrible for building an emotional connection, getting into a real conversation, transforming a stranger into a girlfriend or lover, showing your personality and qualities, or growing or maintaining attraction.

If you use it for these things, you will miss the mark again and again. You won't even get better at hitting the mark in the dark. You'll just waste a lot of bullets, time, and patience. If you want to protest and tell me "No, Chase, that isn't so!" keep reading, and within a few chapters, I bet I'll have changed your mind... or at least have given you something new to chew on.

Regardless, setting up a date must be the primary objective of your texts. Using it for anything else distracts from your core objective and slashes the odds you'll ever make it to your port of call.

#6: Girls Talk Because They Like to Talk

Unless you're incredibly talkative, my guess is you don't spend a great deal of time in long text chats with your male friends. Nor do you likely have these with a girl who's already your girlfriend.

Most men only get into these long conversations with girls they're pursuing.

And those men assume that the girl knows what the deal is. "Obviously, I wouldn't talk to her this much if I didn't want to date her!" the guy thinks. "So, again, obviously she must know this, and, also obviously, her texting back to me is an implicit go-ahead to proceed forward! She's telling me to continue courting her!"

22

There're a lot of assumptions in there... and they're mostly incorrect.

As socially astute as most women are (compared to most men, anyway), they are not mind readers. They know you want something when you text clueless boring questions or endless conversations or large amounts of really, incredibly witty and interesting stuff... they just won't know what it is you want.

And here's the thing: most women love talking! They will talk to you just for the sake of talking. And they'll love it. Many girls will be happy to text back and forth with you all day... and not just you.

They do it with their girlfriends. They do it with their frenemies. They do it with the other eight guys who are chasing them and texting them all day long, too.

You're there talking, thinking it's just about in the bag, because she's so willing to chat with you. And she's there talking... to you, her best friend, her girlfriend, and a gaggle of guys just as gabby over text with her as you.

This isn't the way to a woman's heart. It's simply a way to help her pass the day.

If you spend time in long text conversations with women, you're wasting your time... and fast becoming more valuable as a texting friend than you are as a potential lover or boyfriend.

#7: Women WANT Men Who Are "Just Friends"

Many men who text women have the "hidden agenda" of wanting to get together with those women. Well, most of the women they text have "hidden agendas" of their own.

Think of Mister CBQG. He isn't texting her "What's up?" because he really is dying to know what's up with her. He doesn't care about that. His real agenda is to maneuver this girl into being his lover or girlfriend. As it is, he just happens to think that texting her clueless boring questions is the best way to do that (it isn't).

Well, take Miss Average Girl... when she replies back to CBQG with "Not much. What's up with you?" she also doesn't really care what's up with him, either. She has her own hidden agenda. Hers, most likely, is to make CBQG into someone she is "**just friends**[8]" with.

How cruel and unfair of her, you say? How demeaning for her to want to take this man and finagle him into the **friend zone**![9] How can she possibly live with herself?

Well, wait just a gosh-darned second there. This guy texting her is also trying to finagle her into wanting him. He isn't being forthright about it. He isn't being upfront. He just thinks if he texts her enough, she'll become his girlfriend.

Meanwhile, she thinks if she texts him enough, he'll become her platonic guy pal.

Why this mismatch of desires between texter and textee? Because girls have a lot of options with men, and multiple positions

---

[8] GirlsChase.com – "Just Friends: A Man's Worst Nightmare"
[9] GirlsChase.com – "How to Get Out of the Friend Zone: A Man's Survival Guide"

that any one of those men might best fill. Girls want men who can be "just friends" for them. Friends increase their security levels and make them feel safer. Girls with guy friends are more likely to get help in times of need. They're more likely to be successful in their lives, careers, and other endeavors. Male friends and supporters provide lots of benefits to girls.

And clearly, if you're a guy texting things like "How's it going?" ...and that's it, you're not exactly Grade A lover or boyfriend material. But you might just make a great friend....

Solution? Don't be ambiguous about why you're texting, and don't beat around the bush. We'll cover this more over the next couple of chapters.

#8: Women Cannot "Get to Know You" Over Text

I know a secret of the CBQGs and ECGs and RIWIGs of the world that they themselves are only half aware of. Want to know what it is?

They're all trying to help girls "get to know them" over text message!

"If I text her enough," they think to themselves, "then she'll really get to know me! And then she'll *have* to date me!"

Bzzt! Wrong. Attraction doesn't work that way.

Furthermore, she cannot get to know you over text messages. The things that make texting feel so appealing as a medium for connection-building (i.e., thinking you can get to know her without ever having to worry about your posture, facial expressions, voice tone, or seeming like you're nervous or don't know what to do) also make it marvelously ineffective for actually getting to know someone (i.e., she can't see your posture or facial expressions, hear your voice tone, or tell whether you are nervous or know what to do).

Want her to get to know you?

Meet her in person.

In Summary...

We've just covered eight mental foundations for texting with girls. These are the mindsets every successful texter has. Without these mindsets, you'll make mistakes that cost you dates and progress. Yet *with* them, you'll find texting gets easier and easier.

If you're brand new, and all this information is new to you, you may ask yourself "Dear God, is texting really this complicated?"

To which I say – nonsense! While we've dived deep into an oft-misunderstood subject, the topic matter *isn't* all that complex. You'll only spend 20 minutes or so on texting with the average girl you meet and set up a date with.

The nuances are in how you think about that texting, and the kinds of text messages you send.

Let's have a quick review of our eight mental foundations:

1. Faulty models are your responsibility to fix, not women's.
2. Phone numbers are easy
3. Emotions don't "stick"
4. People want you to reduce their cognitive loads... not pile on
5. You must keep your eye on the ball (i.e., your purpose for texting)
6. Girls talk because they like to talk
7. Women WANT men who are "just friends"
8. Women cannot "get to know you" over text

In the next chapter, I'll introduce you to a simple structure you can use to send the first text to a girl. I'll also arm you with a text "skeleton" you can follow to get girls you take numbers from out on dates. Finally, we'll cover a few general tips for texting to get you started on the right foot.

3

How to Text a Girl

Your Objective in Texting

Let's start with the basics and strategy of text messaging girls. This is what'll drive how you structure messages and how you view texting in general.

Most of the men whose text conversations I see have a real slipshod approach: they text girls with no clear aim. I'm not sure how they expect directionless, objective-free texts to lead to anything much, but hey, I remember the days when I was a lot less effective with texting, and all this felt like a big black question mark to me then, so I commiserate.

We'll shine a little light on texting then, and get you pointed in the right direction. You will only ever have two objectives when texting, and they should never overlap. Here are your objectives in texting girls: (1) build rapport and comfort, or (2) set up a meet.

Number 2 (set up a meet) is your core objective. And the rapport-building or comfort-building you do in #1 must be in service to making #2 a reality. Beyond that, these two objectives are it. Nevertheless, I've discovered a lot of guys who text include a pseudo-objective... something like "keep texting her, then fish around to somehow get a date."

This horrible, atrocious quasi-objective leads men to send all kinds of half-baked text messages – messages that leave a girl to stare at her phone and ask herself "Why the heck is he texting me this?" All messages like this do is torpedo a guy's efforts to win this new girl over.

Thumbs down for the pseudo-objective. If you do that, stop immediately.

Back to our real objectives. When you send text messages, a woman should know immediately what your objective is. And if you recall our two objectives, they are: (1) build rapport and comfort, or (2) set up a meet.

You want her to be able to tell right away what the text is about. The reason you do not want overlap is because once you mix date requests with chit-chat, it gets messy.

That's when you have a guy fish around as he builds rapport, feeling around for some way to transition into asking her out. Don't fall into this trap; keep your objectives separate. Either you text her to build rapport, or you text her to set up a meet.

Some dos and do nots. **Don't** beat around the bush. **Don't** text without an objective. **Don't** send lots and lots of texts. **Don't** get wordy or longwinded. **Do** be direct and straightforward. **Do** text with your objective in mind. **Do** send a handful of well-planned texts. **Do** be precise and concise.

You will always be trying either to build rapport and comfort, or set up a meet. That's all; those are your text objectives when you text a girl you like.

Warm Texting and Cold Texting

One stop into the land of definitions before we continue. I want to differentiate between warm and cold texting, because it's an important distinction. So let's define these terms.

Warm texting is when you text a girl who is thinking about you or expecting to hear from you at the time you text her.

Cold texting is when you text a girl who is not thinking about you or expecting to hear from you when you text her.

Why the distinction? Because you're going adjust your tone to match how ready she is to talk to you. I'll give you a pair of examples:

First, imagine you're off to meet a male coworker for lunch. You're friendly with him but not super close. He texts you: "Just parked. Grab a table yet?" It may be the first text he's sent you all day, but it feels normal because you expected to hear from him.

Now let's say it's 10 AM the next day. You're slogging through some work you don't want to do. Actually, you'd rather be back in bed. You get a text from that same coworker; this one reads: "Just had my second cup of Joe. How's your morning?" To a very social person, it might be cool to get this text... but most people will find this one strange and intrusive; it comes out of the middle of nowhere. They wonder "Why did he text me? What does he want?"

That's the difference between warm and cold texts. The first one – where you planned to meet your coworker – was normal, because you need to figure out when and where to meet.

The second one, though – where'd that come from? This isn't a guy you're super close with. Is he trying to be friends with you? Does he want something from you? Does he have some kind of man-crush on you? Those are the kind of confused questions that pop into your head when a cold text isn't structured right. Structure it wrong, and it can seem like it just came in out of the blue.

How to Structure Your Texts

When you send your first message in a new text conversation, there are a few parts you always want to include. For our purposes, a new text conversation (with a cold text) begins any time the old conversation had a natural end. No exceptions, even if you just talked to her over the phone. It's still a new conversation even if you just changed mediums.

The elements to include in a new text conversation are: (a) greeting, (b) her name, (c) a piece of new information, and (d) something that shows consideration for her.

Each of these plays a big part in the "feel" of the text. Here's what a complete first text with all the elements looks like:

"Gabby, hey. Running a bit behind, sorry. Will be there closer to 2:30. Still cool?"

So we have:

(a) **The greeting:** "hey"
(b) **Her name:** "Gabby"
(c) **Some information:** "Running a bit behind" – "will be there closer to 2:30"
(d) **A little consideration:** "sorry" – "Still cool?"

Also, the fact that you texted to let her know you'd be late in the first place – that also counts as consideration.

In certain cases, we can drop the greeting and it still feels okay, especially if the text is a warm text. So in the example above, we could drop the greeting (hey), and it's still okay, because she expects you to handle logistical issues in the run up to the date. Usually, though, you will want to include the greeting – it increases the chance you'll get a response (Nakajima, 2014).

Next, you should always use a girl's name in the first message of a new text conversation. This trips a mental trigger that reassures her that you're talking to her. Text, phone, and email just don't feel that personal when you don't use the other person's name. I highly, highly recommend that you do.

My text message conversations always start with a name:

"Hey Lily, hope your weekend was good =)"

"Katie, morning!"

"Hi Melanie!"

Always a greeting, and always a name.

For a time, I shied away from exclamation points and emoticons (smileys, winks, etc.) as being too "cutesy." And indeed, women do use them a lot more (Ogletree, Fancher, & Gill, 2014). Me, I thought they made my texts too silly. Instead, I just used periods and trusted girls would get it. Turned out this was wrong. Texts are just far too low context a medium to not use exclamations and emoticons.

Exclamation points and emoticons have more upside than downside. They'll do good things for you in texts, and help compensate for the missing context of the medium (i.e., no voice tone, body language, etc.).

If all you do is use periods, your messages look like this:

> "Hi Jim. Hope your week has been good. Feels like mine's never going to end."

If I get a message like this from a girl, it makes me assume the girl's a total downer; she sounds dour and whiny. I'm scared that if I meet her, she'll suck me into negative topics or she'll get clingy and dependent if we get together.

Interestingly, researchers have even found people rate text messages that end in periods, like the one above, as less sincere as texts without them (Gunraj, Drumm-Hewitt, Dashow, Upadhyay, & Klin, 2016).

Now compare that earlier message to this:

> "Hi Lawrence! Hope your week has been good :) Feels like mine's never going to end..!"

Doesn't that feel so much fresher and more vivid and lively! I can't wait to see this girl. Same exact message, just different punctuation at the end of the sentences. She's a breath of cool air. Our texts (as men) won't be quite that bouncy, since we won't be texting the same way girls text... but it'll be close.

Texting is one of those mediums in which you've got to choose. In this case, the choice is between masculine and negative, or feminine and positive. I'll choose feminine and positive and trust in my real life masculinity to plow under any worries of my texts being too cute. I suggest you do, too. Even with these added elements, texting still feels less natural than face-to-face communication (Skovholt, Grønning, & Kankaanranta, 2014). You can't much afford to do without them and suffer an even more unnatural feel.

One further note on text structure: that's grammar. How grammatically correct should you be?

The challenge with grammar is to be loose enough to seem casual, but not so sloppy that you seem ignorant. Exactly what this means will differ by subculture, country, continent, and era. As such, I can't tell you exactly what grammar to use... because it might well be the wrong grammar for your age or where you live! I will say this, though: your aim with grammar must be to make your text persona match your in-person persona as much as possible.

Text works best as an extension of the individual. Thus, if you've got a nice office job and you dress well and seem excellent, you won't want to text her:

"Wat up bae, wld u lyk get sum drank w/ me?"

Even if you're the local crack dealer, you want cleaner grammar than this. In general, slang is harder to understand... and the harder your texts are to understand, the less she will read and respond to them. Remember, mental loads. Casualness as a stylistic choice *is* good; it's the urge to go too far into too much shorthand you must avoid.

So far, we've talked greetings, grammar, names, and punctuation. Now let's talk about the other two elements to include in all new text conversations: information and consideration.

The information you share is the "point" of the text; it's the reason why you texted. The consideration is the "bond" in the text; it's your way to show care and consideration for this girl.

You must create the right emotions when you text her, because without that, you're sunk. If she's confused about why you sent the text (information is missing or irrelevant), or she feels like it's cold and you aren't focused so much on her (lack of consideration), she'll have confused or bad feelings tied to the text correspondence and be less likely to respond positively, or at all.

Information might be:

"Sitting here in gridlock... this city has the worst traffic ever!"

"Had the most amazing shrimp of my life last night... I can still taste it."

"Thinking we need to get together some time soon."

Consideration might be:

"How's your week looking?"

"How was your test?"

"What's your schedule looking like this week?"

You'll notice I recommend you use "What's your week look like?" themed texts a lot. That's because I find it a great, open-ended question to both: (a) get a girl to talk about anything fun, different, or interesting she's got going on or coming up, and (b) set up logistics for us to meet up.

And, as you'll see in just a moment, I'm going to have you be direct about dates and not waste much time on niceties.

Here's what our text messages to these gals look like fully assembled:

> "Hey Lily, hope your weekend was good =) Sitting here in gridlock... this city has the worst traffic ever! How's your week looking?"

> "Katie, morning! Had the most amazing shrimp of my life last night... I can still taste it. How was your test?"

> "Hi Melanie! Thinking we need to get together some time soon. What's your schedule looking like this week?"

These are cool, fun, personal, and upbeat, and will almost always get responses. How she receives your texts is influenced partly by the initial impression you made on the girl you're sending texts to, of course, and partly by precedent (e.g., if your initial impression was not good for whatever reason, or if you've already set **bad precedent**[10] in your correspondence where you text her but she ignores your text, a good text now may be too little too late), but generally, structured this way, you'll almost always hear back from

---

[10] GirlsChase.com – "Dating and Relationship Precedent: Why It's So Very Important"

women, and they'll almost always be at least somewhat warm and expansive in their replies.

How to Text a Girl to Build Rapport

I recommend you send an initial text message to a girl one to four hours after first meeting her. If you met her toward the end of the night in a bar or nightclub, on the street, or at a party, one or two hours later is okay if you're just about to head to bed.

This initial text is to break the communication *ice*. You want her comfortable talking with you. The importance here is that you want her comfortable *communicating* with you... but remember you aren't trying to get to know her this way. That kind of comfort, as we discussed last chapter, only happens in person.

The catch with communication comfort is: the longer you wait, the more awkward the first contact will be (whether text or call). So text within one to four hours to prevent any awkwardness or expectation settling in. This way, you establish rapport via text message right away.

All you need to do to break the text message ice is send a simple text like:

"Glad to meet a fellow traveler :) -Frank"

or

"Happy to run into you tonight :) -Tommy"

So you give her: (a) a goodwill statement to let her know you're glad you met her, (b) a smiley face to convey warmth and good feelings, and (c) your name.

This serves the following purposes:

It establishes rapport. You've fast moved to establish rapport via text message and removed awkwardness or expectation. When you text or call later, it will be much more natural.

It confirms you like and remember her. Sometimes guys take a girl's phone number and get weird or never text or call at all. A girl can be fearful about whether you actually like her or intend to get in touch again. Or, if you feel you might seem like one of those Jekyll/Hide guys who's cool in person but creepy over text, give her a (brief) goodwill statement with accompanying smiley, and you'll set her mind at ease.

It gives her your name. When you've been at this for a while, you develop a talent for remembering everyone's name, because you get so used to meeting lots and lots of new people that it just becomes routine. I have fun when I meet a group of eight or ten people, get all their names, then go back and tell them all what their names are, and everyone's amazed. Yet most girls are not so talented, and they may well forget your name no matter how much they like you or how much you connect. This can downright embarrass a girl – so much so sometimes that she can't bear to talk to you for the shame of it. Sign your name at the end of that first text and you remove any chance of her feeling dumb or ashamed.

To build rapport, I'll fire off that initial text, then not get in contact with the girl at all the next day. I will reestablish rapport the day after (unless she reaches out to me first). At that time, you can fire off a few rapport-building texts to get her comfortable chatting with you. These should follow the structure we covered earlier, at least for the first text or two.

Some general outlines on rapport-building texts:

Be concise. Shorter texts get far more replies than longwinded ones.

Stay positive. No one likes a downer; bring good, positive energy to your texts. Girls should look forward to texts from you. Let them dread texts from the boring, life-sucking guys... while you light up their days.

Keep it to a few texts. Unless you get in a spectacular text conversation with a girl, you'll want to keep it to three to ten texts sent, generally.

Watch the time. It's okay to vary your response times, but don't reply too much more quickly to a girl's texts than she replies to yours until you get pretty advanced, lest you risk looking like you're waiting by the phone for her reply with nothing better to do. Once you're advanced, you can play around with varying response times. Sometimes I'll reply within minutes to a girl's text; other times it might take me hours. Usually that's more because I'm busy than anything else... but building variance into your response time is a good thing to do.

How to Text a Girl to Arrange a Meet

This is the real meat of this chapter, and the most important part of it. I hardly spend the time to build rapport over text these days; I usually go straight to the date setup. If you prefer to build comfort and rapport first, I suggest a rough schedule like this: (a) initial text several hours after you first meet and grab her number; (b) rapport-building texts two days after the first meet/number grab; (c) arrange the date four to five days after the first meet/number grab.

That's all you need. Less even. I often skip the rapport building these days unless I think a girl needs it. Instead, I move to set up the meet the day after I've traded numbers with a girl, or the next day after that. You don't need to talk to her for weeks before she's ready to meet up with you; you don't need to win her over.

You just need to get her out.

Back in my days as a tire salesman, my old boss asked if I knew what the telephone was for. I answered, "To sell the customer on a tire?"

He said, "No. It's to get them in the store. A good, seasoned salesman like Jim can sell a customer on a tire over the phone. But even Jim knows not to push too hard to try to sell over the phone unless he can tell that's what the customer wants. All I want you to do with the telephone is to get the customer in the store. Phone sales are an uphill battle. But get them in the store, and then they've come into the store; they've decided this is where they'll buy their tires, and they're committed. More likely than not they'll buy the tire. You stand a much better chance to sell the customer when they're here in front of you than when you have them on the phone. Get them in the store."

I took that to heart and made it my priority with every phone call I answered from a customer. Whenever I found myself on the phone, my priority was to get them in the store.

I forgot this lesson for a while when I was first learning how to do well with girls. I'd have these long, drawn-out phone/text back-and-forths that spanned weeks or months. Sometimes I'd finally meet the girl, and sometimes nothing would come of it. It was about as effective as hammering nails with a Nerf ball. I hated the phone in those days. I had better luck just taking a girl home the night I met her.

But then I remembered "get them in the store." Translated to dating, it's "get them out with you."

So I stopped trying to sell myself over the phone, and just started using it as a logistical tool to set up dates. My success soared. I've hardly even used phone calls at all for years. Heck, in the first fifteen days of this year, I slept with four new girls... every one of them on first dates... and every one of those dates was coordinated via text message. My secret? "Get them out with you."

Every guy I teach this method to gets dates with girls who normally wouldn't come out. How's it work? There are three elements to a meet-up text: (1) be warm, (2) offer value, and (3) keep your eye on the ball. The ball being the meet, of course.

The value you offer can be something cool or fun with her, or it may just be leading her to what she wants to do (meet you). Sometimes girls will ask side questions like "How was your day?" Answer these questions, but continue to push toward the meet. Don't get sidetracked. Here's what an example conversation might look like as you forge ahead toward setting up a meet:

> **You:** Lisa, hey! Let's figure out a time to grab a bite. How's this weekend looking for you?

Her: This weekend's okay, sure! How are you??

You: I'm good! Why don't we do Saturday at 1 PM? We can meet at Main St Station Exit 2 and go from there. Cool?

Her: Okay!

You: Awesome. See you Sat ;)

And bam! that's all it takes. Note that when she asked how you were, you didn't get sidetracked; you kept your eye on the ball (the meet). A pal of mine recently fell into that trap and swerved off course. He ended up not meeting a girl who wanted to meet him, because he got sucked into irrelevant questions. Keep your eye on the ball and continue to push – gently, calmly, and in a socially savvy way – for the meet. Then, **plan a good date**[11], make it a **simple date**[12], and she's as good as yours.

See my book *How to Plan a Date: Girls Chase Guides* for a list of the best structures to use for dates with girls... not to mention how to lead those dates to sex and a relationship.

What to Expect as a Beginner

Some of what you can expect as a texting beginner:

The icebreaker text means you get more "warm" numbers and fewer dead numbers when you text within the next day or two.

---

[11] GirlsChase.com – "Date Templates: Minimize Confusion, Maximize Returns"
[12] GirlsChase.com – "Simplify Your Dates"

The four text structure elements make girls suddenly respond a LOT better to your texts.

You start to have girls want to communicate with you much more over text.

And you get more comfortable asking girls out on dates.

The biggest gains come from adding in any missing elements and getting to the point (i.e., setting up the date). Once you do these, the new dates and lays start to roll in.

What to Expect at Intermediate

Some of what you can expect as a texting intermediate:

As your aims get clearer (i.e., get her out on dates), things start to move faster

And as things move faster, you turn more of the phone numbers you get into dates, sex, and girlfriends

Girls start to text you if you don't text them soon enough, and sometimes ask YOU out

You begin to have an intuitive grasp of "texting psychology"

By this point, the structure is second nature and you don't have to think about it. Your reply timing is expert. And you have a sense for how to intrigue girls without getting sidetracked. Dates are a lot easier to set up and pull off.

What to Expect When Advanced

Some of what you can expect as an advanced texter:

You start to bend some of the rules a bit, and do things like text girls to meet up the same day you grab numbers from them (and you see "yes").

You begin to flake more as you get busier and have scheduling conflicts; most girls are willing to wait for you and happy to reschedule.

Your texting becomes even more minimalist. You stop almost all the cutesy stuff and focus entirely on getting girls out on dates.

You can pick up and text girls you haven't talked to in ages, and more often than not they respond (and agree to a meet).

You're now seeing the latticework and can climb around and adjust things to suit your fancy. You know the rules well enough now that you know where the trapdoors and secret passageways are. And you're able to get girls excited and willing to meet you and come almost anywhere with just one or two precise texts.

In Summary...

In this chapter, I gave you the meat and potatoes of texting. I introduced you to the two possible objectives your texts can have: (1) build rapport and comfort, or (2) set up a meet.

And I noted that Objective #1 only works if it is in service of Objective #2. The reason to stick to these objectives is because you want clarity. She needs to know right away what your texts are about.

The big don'ts in texting are: don't beat around the bush; don't text without an objective; don't send lots and lots of texts; and don't get wordy or longwinded. The big dos in texting are: do be direct and straightforward; do text with your objective in mind; do send a handful of well-planned texts; and do be precise and concise.

We discussed the difference between cold texts and warm texts. And we looked at why it's vital to format your texts carefully if they're going to be cold. Send her a too-familiar cold text, and you can sink your chances. You must send the right text to warm her up.

Then, I gave you my structure for the most effective first texts. That structure contains four parts: (a) greeting, (b) her name, (c) a piece of new information, and (d) something that shows consideration for her.

We talked about some structural elements of texting: emoticons, grammar, and punctuation. And I gave you the best approaches to use on each of them.

Finally, we talked about how to structure texts for the two objectives: building rapport and comfort, or arranging the meet. I gave you the three elements to a meet-up text: (1) be warm, (2) offer value, and (3) keep your eye on the ball. The ball being the meet, of course. And I gave some examples for each type of text.

Now that you've got the basic framework around which to build your texts, it's time to get your hands real dirty. The next chapter gives you the deep mechanics: all the detail, nuance, how-tos, and what's-thats. This is where we take you from competent in texting... to really technically brilliant at it. All your technical questions (for the most part) get their answers in Chapter 4.

4

Opening up the Hood

Even More Mechanics

In the last chapter, we armed you with a simple process to follow whenever you send girls texts. And two chapters back, we covered eight ground rules to texting with girls. In case you forgot what those ground rules are, they include the realizations that:

1. Faulty models are your responsibility to fix, not women's
2. Phone numbers are easy
3. Emotions don't "stick"
4. People want you to reduce their cognitive loads... not pile on
5. You must keep your eye on the ball (i.e., your purpose for texting)
6. Girls talk because they like to talk
7. Women WANT men who are "just friends"
8. Women cannot "get to know you" over text

Now that you've got your foundations set, and you've got the basic skeleton, you're ready to dive into the mechanics. These are the real nuances, the nuts and bolts... the nitty gritty of how to text girls and actually have it go the way you want it to, almost without fail.

This is the chapter you've been waiting for.

#1: Propose the Date Before You Ask for the Number!

This one's so important that I put an exclamation point on it.

A lot of newer guys skip this step. It just feels easier to ask for the number. After all, if she says "no," all she's rejecting is giving you her phone number, right? It's not like she's rejecting a date with you or anything!

But that's preposterous. If she refuses you her number, by extension she refuses all future possibilities of you and her doing anything together, ever. That includes dates.

When you go to take her phone number, you must ask for the date FIRST!

Not only does this actually make it easier to get phone numbers from girls... it also makes things much easier when you sit down to figure out how to correspond with her afterward.

Better still, it makes you look confident. If you had a chance to ask a girl out in person, then didn't, and waited to do it over text later, she may assume you lacked the courage to ask her in person... and thus be not worth meeting again in person (ANI, 2010).

I'm convinced that if men started to ask girls on dates before they asked for phone numbers, CBQGs and ECGs would become extinct. And RIWIGs would become an endangered species.

Here's ALL you have to do:

> **Her:** [mid-conversation wherever you met] ... so then I totally got out of there before things could get even worse!
>
> **You:** That's hilarious.
>
> **Her:** I know, right? I thought I was going to die for a minute! That girl was crazy!
>
> **You:** Hey, I'm going to have to jet in a minute, but we should grab a drink or some food this week or early next. What's your schedule like?
>
> **Her:** Oh, I don't know, I'll have to take a look. I think I'm free on Sunday.
>
> **You:** Cool, I'll text you. What's your number?
>
> **Her:** 619...

Isn't that way easier than the big productions most men make of trying to get phone numbers?

Furthermore, doesn't that make it way more straightforward when you want to text her later? Don't you know exactly what you need to do now?

If you want my opinion, you ought to open up your phone right now and delete every number you took from girls you didn't ask out beforehand. Or, if you'd rather take a stab before you delete those numbers, text every single one of them right now with something like:

> Hey [name], I just stumbled across this really cool little café in [area] with the most amazing hot chocolates. I totally want to take you there - want to grab a chocolate and a bite to eat with me sometime this week / next week?

Any girl you get "yeah, sure" or a "how about we do XYZ instead" from, hang onto; you can work with that. Any girl you get a "no, I really can't" or a "sorry, I'm busy" from, just delete.

Now you're starting fresh.

And every number you get from here on out, before you get it, make absolutely sure you've gotten it in the context of doing so in order to set up and plan for a date.

No more figuring out what to text her. No more pacing back and forth in your room deciding what you should say.

Now you know what to say: you're going to text her to find out when she wants to meet.

#2: Use an Icebreaker Text

We talked about this in the last chapter, but I want to harp on it again. The longer you wait after getting a girl's number to text her, the weirder it starts to feel. There are a variety of "weirdness" factors that come into play: she wonders when you're going to text her, or she forgets about you altogether; plus you build things up in your head and get awkward, or you push things off so long that she wonders why you're texting a week later.

Solution? **You need to break the ice[13].**

Breaking the ice gives you the freedom to be more natural later. The awkwardness of wondering whether the conversation will be normal and comfortable over text is gone. This new girl knows that you are going to follow up with her.

Breaking the ice sets the tone for you to text women later on without having to introduce yourself or remind her of when she met you. That's because you cement those initial feelings while they're still fresh in her mind.

A typical icebreaker text looks like this:

> **You:** Wonderful to meet you, new friend :) -Steve

or

> **You:** Glad to have met you :) -Steve

You **do not** tell her you "like" her, qualify her (as in "You're a really cool/amazing/neat girl!"), ask her any questions, or propose a date.

You **do** keep it very short, use the word "friend" if possible, and sign your name.

It's short because this is just to break the ice and reassure her you aren't one of these guys who are in love and writing her novels already. You communicate from the outset that you adhere to the **Law of Least Effort[14]**. And you show her that meeting a new girl

---

[13] GirlsChase.com – "How to Break the Ice: 5 Surefire Ways to Entice Her"
[14] GirlsChase.com – "The Law of Least Effort"

isn't a big deal to you... like it is for many men, who are quick to deluge girls with volumes and volumes of texts just after meeting.

You use **friend** where possible because you want to confuse and intrigue her a little bit. Do you like her or not? She thinks you do... but now you're using this ambiguous term. Ambiguity is one of the properties of text, and it's one you can turn to your advantage (Meenagh, 2015). So you use this, and she's guessing... she's intrigued. Most guys state verbal interest right away and kill the intrigue, excitement, and mystery. Women don't want men like that... they want men who'll keep them guessing and who won't let them know how the story ends – right up until it does.

If a girl seems super into you and seems to view you as far higher status than herself, you may elect to drop "friend"... so as not to send her into **auto-rejection**[15], thinking she can't get you.

And you sign your name because she may well have forgotten it. If you don't include your name, and she forgets it, she's either going to feel awkward that she's forgotten, and not respond, or feel awkward that she's forgotten, and have to ask you. But if you include your name, then no matter what, she won't be able to dismiss you by saying "Who's this?" even if she might've been tempted to otherwise. This is an all-too-common reason women use to brush guys off if they're on the fence.

Very, *very* occasionally, you will get a girl writing "Who?" back after your initial text, even if it's only a few hours later, and even if you've signed your name. This is almost always a brush-off attempt; don't respond back by telling her who it is.

---

[15] GirlsChase.com articles – "Secrets to Getting Girls: Staying Out of Auto-Rejection"

When I get something like this from a girl – it's rare, but it still happens – I usually just delete the number as no good and move on. If she's THAT disinterested, or her memory of you is THAT poor, you're almost certainly not going to get her out again. You can still play around with numbers like this for practice if you want... just don't expect to get anything. But this is pretty rare, and unless you do tons of approaches, you may never see it. Just keep signing your name.

When should you send an icebreaker text? About 1 to 4 hours after meeting her.

You can sometimes go sooner, although 30 minutes is about the soonest you want to do this. If you wait too much longer than 3 or 4 hours, you're getting into awkward territory... so break the ice before then.

And don't worry about getting a response; you're texting to break the ice, not open a dialogue. You'll still get dates and lovers from women who don't respond to your icebreaker texts. It's just icing on the cake if they do respond.

#3: Don't Wait Too Long

You know those old dating guides that tell you to wait 3 days or a week or whatever it is before even calling a girl?

Throw those handbooks in the garbage pail; they'll do you no good here.

Run things based off how your interaction went when you met her. Use these metrics:

If she was excited about you when you met her, text her to set up the date the next day, or even that day if you met her in the afternoon or morning. You'll find you can set up dates for the same or following day with girls who were excited to meet you. In fact, these are always your best bets... the emotions are fresh, the desire is hot, and you create that whirlwind romance that most girls dream of experiencing all their lives.

If she was just nice toward you when you met her, text her 1 or 2 days later. 1 or 2 days is enough time for her to "make up her mind" whether she wants to see you again... but not so much time she'll have lost interest entirely. If you wait longer than that, she may just say "Ah, I wasn't that interested. Never mind."

Remember the maxim on here: **move faster**[16]. If you wait too long, some guy who knows this rule better than you will beat you to the punch. Or life may intervene with any number of other unexpected obstacles.

Strike while the iron is hot, or content yourself with an uneven blade (i.e., not such good odds to land her).

#4: Don't Beat Around the Bush

Like we discussed two chapters back, if you slink around and try to trick girls into liking you and dating you, girls will respond in turn... and slink around to try to trick you into being platonic friends with them.

---

[16] GirlsChase.com – "Secrets to Getting Girls: Move Faster"

One good turn deserves another, says Aesop.

That's why all the "text her until she's ready for a date" strategies don't work that well. You can't text your way into somebody's heart.

You've got to do that in person.

If you're sending texts that don't suggest a meet-up in the first text (aside from an icebreaker text), then you are beating around the bush.

Why?

Because she knows you want something, but you aren't saying what it is.

Catherine knows you weren't sitting around at 2 PM when the urge to find out how her day was going just randomly struck you out of the blue. "Gee," you said to yourself, "I know my day's going swell... but how's the day of that girl I met at the coffee shop last weekend going?"

She knows you didn't just send a text message to Randy the maintenance guy and Stefo your old college roommate asking them how *their* days are going. You messaged *her*... because you *want* something.

But you're beating around the bush and not telling her what it is.

If you get a message like this from someone:

> **Person:** Hey man, how's your day going? Mine's pretty good; just had a great club sandwich.

... you know this person wants something, and is going to ask you for something.

And if you're not especially inclined to grant favors, you're likely to ignore it. Or you may give a perfunctory reply to discourage him or her from asking about it.

You also perceive this behavior as weak.

So don't do this. It moves you further away from *attractive* and *date-worthy*, not closer.

Instead, your initial message of a conversation is best structured like this:

> **You:** Hope the rest of your weekend was great, Catherine! I ended up taking a trip to Bear Mountain last minute with some friends... It was both surprising and awesome. Let's grab that lunch we talked about later this week - when's good for you schedule-wise?

Nothing hidden. No beating around the bush. Just some light pleasantries, and then you spell out what you want clear as day.

It's short, brief, and straight to the point – and doesn't make her wonder at all what you're after. Women respond better and more consistently to this than any other texting style you'll ever use ("respond" here means setting up a date with you, as opposed to entering into an engaging-but-ultimately-unproductive text banter/conversation, which seems to be most men's idea of a girl being "responsive").

#5: Keep Texts Short

Your first message to kick off a new conversation can be a little bit of an exception to this... just so you have enough space to fit the pleasantries in before the ask.

Other than that, though, your texts should not be much longer than the last message you received from her. If your texts are much longer than hers are, you violate **sprezzatura**[17]... and look **try-hard**[18] in the process.

That means if she sends you:

> **Her:** Hey Charlie, didn't hear from you last week :) What's up?

Don't send her:

> **You:** Hey Marlene, sorry I didn't reply sooner! I was actually SUPER busy last week traveling to meet some new business clients. It's really cool stuff but a lot of work. Did get to see the Cirque du Soleil when I was in Vegas though... Wait until you hear about THAT one! Anyway, what've you been up to? Hope all's been well. We still on for lunch this Thursday?

That's *okay*, and it's good stuff, but it's too much as a reply to a short text. If you've been cool with her, she'll just view it as you being enthusiastic about an awesome week. If you haven't, she'll view it as you trying to force a connection.

---

[17] GirlsChase.com – "Sprezzatura, Effort, and Investing"
[18] GirlsChase.com – "Are You Trying Too Hard? Stop Trying. Start Succeeding"

Instead, send her this:

> **You:** Sorry Marlene, I was up to my eyeballs last week :/
> Tell you about it when I see you. Still lunch on Thursday,
> yes?

On the other hand, if a girl sends you a wall of text, don't send her "Cool" or "Let's do it" as a response. She'll feel awkward and as though you aren't as interested in her as she is in you.

You want her to feel your interest levels closely match hers. To do that, you'll want to keep your text messages short – and similar in length.

#6: Ask and Share Something Personal to Relate

Imagine last week you met a guy at a networking meeting. He seemed like an okay guy. Not amazing, no great connections that could help you land an awesome new job... nothing like that. Just an okay guy. This new acquaintance asked you if you'd like to grab a beer sometime and shoot the breeze, and you said sure, why not, and gave the guy your phone number.

Now imagine it's a few days later and you've largely forgotten about this guy. Then he sends you a text message. Which of these three is the most likely to get a "yes" response out of you?

Text Message A:

> **Acquaintance:** Tim, want to grab that beer we talked about
> tonight?

Text Message B:

> **Acquaintance:** Hey Tim, how'd that audit go? Want to grab that beer we talked about tonight?

Text Message C:

> **Acquaintance:** Hey Tim, how'd that audit go? I've got one of those myself coming up... what a pain. Want to grab that beer we talked about tonight?

If you're like most people, and your time is sacred (if your time is more of a free-for-all, go look up the 1922 article entitled "Why I Quit Being So Accommodating"), your reactions will be something like a woman's reaction to the same messages if they came from a guy she met informally a few days ago. So now let's use your own reactions to the above texts and jump into the mind of a woman and see if you can now empathize with her:

Her reaction to Message A:

> "Wait, who is this guy? Do I really want to give him my evening?"

Obviously not a reaction you want.

Her reaction to Message B:

> "Is this guy trying to butter me up because he wants something?"

Also not a reaction you want.

Her reaction to Message C:

> "This guy seems like not a bad guy. I can probably afford a quick drink."

Now you're on the right track.

So, what's the difference? Message C is personal and relates to you.

There's a distinct formula here: (a) greet her with her name (yes, this is important, casual texters); then (b) ask her how something in her life went; next, (c) relate to that, and share something similar from your life; and finally, (d) ask her to meet you, with a subtle reminder that she already agreed to.

The name is to reinforce in her mind that this is a *personal* text, and not a mass text.

Asking her about something personal is to get her to start relating.

Sharing your own experience in the same vein as the question is to finish up the relating by showing her that the two of you are not so different.

Asking her to meet you is getting to the point, and mentioning (in passing! Don't put it out directly, unless you want to look like you don't think she's going to say yes) that she's already said "yes" makes her remember why she said "yes"...and makes her a lot more likely to say it again this time around.

Keep it personal.

#7: Avoid Asking
Too Many Questions / Irrelevant Questions

This one's simple. Don't go around asking girls weird/irrelevant, or even lots of, questions via text. A simple "How's/How'd your X going/go?" is a formality that makes things more personal. A question like "Shall we grab that coffee we discussed this week?" is necessary so a woman doesn't feel like you're unilaterally trying to decide for her. "Let's grab that coffee we discussed this week" is too imposing and is likely to lead to resistance.

Both of these questions are good.

But they're just two questions: (1) a personal "formality" type question, and (2) a "buy in" type question about the date.

Other than those two, that's it. No other questions – everything else is irrelevant.

You'll talk to her more when you see her in person. No **deep diving**[19] via text, my friend; much of its effect is lost without the body language and **nonverbal communication**[20].

#8: Ignore Unhelpful Questions and Topics

Sometimes a girl may be on the fence about whether she wants you as a date or a friend. When this is the case, she'll often try to wedge unhelpful or distracting questions or topics into a text conversation.

---

[19] GirlsChase.com – "Secrets to Getting Girls: The Art of the Deep Dive"
[20] GirlsChase.com – "Nonverbal Communication"

She does this to slow things down or steer you away from "date-like" activities and toward "friend-like" ones.

That looks like this:

> **You:** Haley, how was your weekend? Hope you got a lot of rest in. I was super lazy all weekend... but sometimes you need weekends like that. Hey, so how about we grab that bite we talked about this week? Let me know what your schedule's looking like and let's get the gears in motion.

> **Her:** Hey Will... omg, my weekend was insane. Waaay too much drinking Saturday night, never doing that again, lol! Lunch? Let me check what I have going on this week. Oh, btw, did you hear about the new club they're opening up downtown next week? It's called "Motown." We should totally go to that! I have a friend who says he can get tickets.

This is where most guys drop the ball. They *feel* like something's wrong here... this girl seems to be calling the shots. It's weird. It doesn't feel completely right saying "Sure, let's go to that club opening..." but they do anyway, because they don't think they have a choice.

They didn't ignore unhelpful stuff. They welcomed it in the front door and left that door open for more to keep pouring in, instead.

Why's this bad? If it's not clear why letting girls lead, going to party dates, and things of that nature are very bad for seduction, see these Girls Chase articles:

- The Real Reason Many Men Can't Get a Girl
- The Sad Tale of "Shopping Guy"
- The Party Date: Don't Do It

Next, when you get hit with unhelpful and distracting topics, just duck and weave:

> **You:** Haley, how was your weekend? Hope you got a lot of rest in. I was super lazy all weekend... but sometimes you need weekends like that. Hey, so how about we grab that bite we talked about this week? Let me know what your schedule's looking like and let's get the gears in motion.
>
> **Her:** Hey Will... omg, my weekend was insane. Waaay too much drinking Saturday night, never doing that again, lol! Lunch? Let me check what I have going on this week. Oh, btw, did you hear about the new club they're opening up downtown next week? It's called "Motown." We should totally go to that! I have a friend who says he can get tickets.
>
> **You:** Oh man, that sounds awesome, though let me take a rain check on Motown! I'm all out of club juice in me lately. There is such a thing as too much clubbing, believe it or not... ;) Well, check your schedule and let me know which day's good for you on grabbing a bite. I've got Wednesday and Thursday free at lunch time, and Saturday free right up until 8 o'clock - let me know if either works!

If the girl just wants you as a friend here, you'll get a negative response back on the date. She'll be "busy" those times, and try to reschedule for some other time. She does this to maintain the advantage and stay in control – which is what she needs to friend zone you.

But if she's on the fence, she'll come back and tell you one of those times works.

Be prepared to have to do a kick-ass job getting some **sexual tension**[21] brewed up when you meet her, though. And have your sprezzatura at full blast. Have both of these in place, and you can escape that "possible friend" mantle she's draped around your neck. Just make sure you move fast!

#9: Use Interesting Language

This one's harder to teach. It's just best if you're well-read and have a little experience writing. If you can pick interesting, colorful language out, it helps make your texts more captivating.

A few colorful phrases to get you started:

- "Shall we" instead of "Would you like to" or "Do you want to"
- "Scoop you" instead of "Pick you up" (in a car, for a date, etc.)
- "Grab [lunch, a drink, etc.]" or "Snag" instead of "Get" or "Have"
- Using verbs instead of nouns (e.g., "I napped" instead of "I took a nap")
- Using active voice ("I got this" instead of "They gave me this")

Colorful language is just more attractive, and makes *you* more attractive, too. Its effects on women mirror those of humor... a display of social intelligence that ups attraction.

---

[21] GirlsChase.com – "Sexual Tension: 7 Ways to Make Women Excited and Randy"

#10: Vary Your Response Frequency

This isn't a problem when you're genuinely busy... when you're involved in a hundred things socially. Or you've got six different women you're seeing. Or you're running your own business. Or you've got a million projects to manage for work. In these cases, your response time naturally varies. It'll be lightning quick sometimes, and glacially slow others.

This is optimal. Girls respond best to men whose response time is unpredictable, but within a certain range. Now, if you always take a day to respond to her, or it happens too much, she'll likely auto-reject. So don't go overboard.

Basically, don't go too extreme in either direction. If a girl always takes an hour to write you back, don't always write her back in 10 minutes. Instead, write her back in 10 minutes one time... and 2 hours the next.

Response times will tend to vary naturally for most busy people. Actually, if you notice that a girl: (a) always texts you back after the same amount of time (e.g., 40 minutes), or (b) always texts you back after the same amount of time that it took you to respond to *her* last text, you know she's playing games with you. Don't call her out on it, just... be mindful.

And play her game back better than she knows how – vary your response times and don't be predictable.

You'll keep her guessing – and intrigued.

#11: Make Seeing You in Person the ONLY Way to Talk with You

Like we said two chapters back, girls talk because they like to talk.

And as you recall, we also discussed that girls WANT guys to "just be (platonic) friends" with.

How does that affect how you text girls?

Simple: **you don't give them what they're looking for over text**.

A girl wants a texting buddy? Great!

That's not you.

A girl wants someone to go into deep conversation with over SMS? Fantastic!

It just isn't you.

She wants someone to send her lots of texts and make her feel special? Outstanding!

But she'll have to find someone else for that.

The *only* thing *you* use text messages for is *getting girls out to meet you IN PERSON*.

If she can get her fill of you via text, the odds of her coming out to meet you drop dramatically lower.

But, if she really likes you... and if she really wants to talk with you... and she *can't get that from you* via text message... and you won't talk to her on the phone much, either...

She WILL meet you.

And once the two of you are there, in person and in the flesh, you can work your magic.

#12: Leave Something Small to Cover, and Send a Pre-Meeting Text

When you set up the actual logistics of a date, it's best to leave some small detail out that you can cover later. While this isn't totally necessary, it's helpful for your pre-meeting text.

You nearly always want to use a **pre-meeting text** for two reasons. The first is you reassure your date that yes, you remember the place and time, and you *will* be there. This nixes any chance of her flaking out of fear of you not showing up. The second is that you give her the opportunity to give you a heads up if *she* intends to flake. This makes sure you don't waste your time going somewhere if she's going to be late or not make it at all.

A pre-meeting text with a pertinent detail you didn't mention earlier will look like this:

> **You:** Hey Cassie! Heading out in 10 minutes; should be there right at 2 PM. I'll meet you at the subway station's South Exit.

A pre-meeting text if you don't have any specific pertinent data to cover will look like this:

> **You:** Hey Cassie! Heading out in 10 minutes; should be there right at 2 PM. I'll grab a seat inside if I'm the first one there.

Either of these work just fine, and both reassure her you're going. Both also remind her to give you a heads up if she isn't going, so you don't waste your time (and get angry/annoyed).

If she does flake, of course, then stay tuned. We'll talk about just what to do two chapters from now.

In Summary...

We just took an under-the-hood look at texting best practices. These are the technical rules to follow to ensure your texts go over well.

Veteran texters figure these rules out organically, on their own. This chapter lets you shortcut the (often long and arduous) trial-and-error method and skip straight to awesome texting.

The mechanics of good texting:

1. Propose the date before you ask for the number
2. Use an icebreaker text
3. Don't wait too long
4. Don't beat around the bush
5. Keep texts short
6. Ask and share something personal to relate
7. Avoid asking too many questions / irrelevant questions
8. Ignore unhelpful questions and topics
9. Use interesting language
10. Vary your response frequency
11. Make seeing you in person the ONLY way to talk to you
12. Leave something small to cover, and send a pre-meeting text

Up next, we'll discuss exactly what to do when a girl doesn't text back... because even the most advanced texter still sometimes has a girl go radio silent. The difference between the advanced texter and everyone else, though, is that he knows how to get her responding again (then, out on a date).

5

What to Do When She Won't Text Back

Girls Not Texting

A Girls Chase reader wrote in:

> I found something strange. Every time I have long
> interactions with a girl in a pick up on the streets, I bomb. I
> mean, she doesn't text back. It reminds me of Murphy's
> Law: if anything can go wrong, IT WILL. I recently
> approached 10 women who gave me attraction signals.
> They touched me, called me cute, called me the most
> interesting person, smiled, were high energy, stayed 20
> minutes, and asked me to text them. I had good
> interactions with them and was smooth and confident. I
> bonded with them and made plans to see them. They
> never texted back, and I don't know why.

I did another experiment where I cut my interaction short to about 3 minutes and asked for the number. Most of the shorter ones agreed on dates and texted back, and note, most of them gave me negative signs first. Is it because women give guys fake "attraction signals?" Why do they seem so much into me at first but never bother to actually get into contact again? It happens so much that when a girl gives me signals that are too good to be true, I can almost predict that I will never hear from her again and I'm always right. I know it sounds counterintuitive but I think the women who give you immediate signals are maybe time wasters? And what are your thoughts, do you find the same?

Brings back memories.

When I started to approach girls a lot more in 2006, I noticed an odd trend. The trend was this: girls I spoke to longer, who seemed more into me... were less likely to ever return calls or texts.

"How bizarre," I thought to myself. "This makes no sense."

The numbers didn't lie. So I did the only logical thing I could think to do: I slashed the time I spent with girls whose phone numbers I intended to grab. I started to only spend a longer time with girls I intended to take home that day or night.

Almost overnight, the problem of girls not texting or calling back all but vanished. But it still left me scratching my head.... Why did spending more time with a girl and having her come to like you more lead to her falling off the face of the Earth and not returning texts and calls later?

Things That Lead to Unreturned Texts and Calls

Think of a girl you met, who you liked, who you spent maybe 30 or 40 minutes talking to in your initial encounter. She was charming, beautiful, exactly your type.

Got her in your head?

Good. Now, if you can, remember how you felt the first time you called her or texted her. Felt pretty darn nervous, didn't you? Heck, maybe you didn't even text or call her at all. I hope that wasn't the case, but there are plenty of guys out there that's happened to... it happened to me. In fact, I almost didn't call a girl who was to become my girlfriend for 2½ years. It was just too scary to dial her number on the phone. I almost didn't talk to her again after the night I met her.

Guess what? Yep: that happens to girls, too.

Now, it isn't always the reason. In fact, it's only one of four main reasons we'll discuss that may cause her to not reply to you. But nervousness and pressure is one of the Big 4 Reasons why girls may not respond.

This one's likely the most surprising reason for a lot of guys, so that's why I chose to lead with it. But there are three other reasons, too. The four reasons girls might not reply to you are:

Too much anticipation/nervousness: if a girl likes you a lot, she can be "too shy to reply." She can put a great deal of pressure on herself to do well with you... or be too jittery to type out a reply or answer your call. She may really, really want to talk to you, yet never end up doing so.

Too much of a state-shift: this one's a little tougher to get your mind around at first, so I'll use an example. Say you met an excited girl at a party, hit it off, and took her phone number. The next day you call her or text her. But now she's low energy and lethargic, and likely not to answer. You are that "wild guy from the party"... but she's not in "party mode" right now. She will look at your message and think to herself: "I can't talk to him right now; it's too much work..." and then just never get back to you.

A bad ending: "The end is important in all things." So goes one of my favorite quotes from the Hagakure. Even if you had a dynamite opener and the majority of the conversation was terrific. If the END is awkward or stale, odds are you won't hear from her again.

She wasn't all that interested: this happens sometimes to everyone. Resist the temptation to attribute every no-response to disinterest. This is what most guys do ("I guess she didn't like me after all"). It's actually quite often one of the other three reasons that's to blame. But sometimes it really is just that she wasn't as interested as she seemed. It happens.

Of these four reasons, #3 and #4 are the easiest to fix.

Number 3 (bad endings) you fix when you get your closing streamlined. Check out my book *How to Ask a Girl Out: a Girls Chase Guide,* or read the GirlsChase.com article on **getting a girl's phone number**[22]. Use these tips and get more practice going for closes, and you'll begin to self-correct and get smoother and more natural with time.

---

[22] GirlsChase.com – "Secrets to Getting Girls: Natural Number Swapping"

Number 4 (she just isn't interested) you fix as you become more attuned to the signals women are giving you. You grow more aware of **how to tell a girl is interested**[23] in you. Then, you plain and simple don't take contact info from girls you know aren't that intrigued.

Number 1 (girls who're too nervous to respond because they really like you) is tougher to correct. You have to minimize nervousness and maximize comfort while you're there in person with her... plus you've got to make sure that the contact you have with her afterward is super warm and friendly. She must feel comfortable responding to you, above all.

Number 2 (girls who have a big mood shift between the time you meet and the time you text) is the hardest to deal with. You have to actually change the way you interact with girls when you meet. If you intend to grab numbers, you must reduce the energy level and get more "real." The goal is that when such a girl gets your text or call later, when they're in a less ribald mood, it won't feel too hard for her to respond.

These four changes may require you to completely overhaul you interactions with girls... especially if you're an energetic, high-energy guy.

The good news, though, is there's a shortcut around all these learning curves. That shortcut is...

---

[23] GirlsChase.com – "How Girls Show Interest"

Spend Less Time with Girls and Get Them Responding More

Sounds counterintuitive, I know, but bear with me on this one.

Less time spent with a girl before you go for her contact information does something special for you. First, it lets you screen out girls who aren't much into you. But it also lets you cut out the bad stuff: girls who get so into you they're too afraid to talk to you later; girls who get used to talking to you in a too-different energy level from their usual energy level; and bad endings to your interactions with girls.

Said another way, less time up front is about as close to a cure-all for the "girls not texting back" problem as you can get.

The girls who are into you right off the bat aren't time wasters. They're not insincere. They may well enjoy the long conversation they have with you... or maybe they're just trying to be polite with someone who took the time to approach and talk to them. It's vital to note the difference between **reactions and results**[24]. The two are different things altogether, and reactions can often be misleading.

A girl's smiles, laughs, and chats with you are reactions. Her moving somewhere with you, or giving you her number when you ask for it fast... those are a few examples of results. Results are what you need, regardless of how promising (or not) your reactions may be.

---

[24] GirlsChase.com — "Reactions from Women, or Results with Women?"

When you ask for the number fast, you get a real result. The girls who like you will happily give theirs. The ones who aren't so inclined will hesitate, or refuse outright.

Very fast way to sift the wheat from the chaff.

When a Girl Doesn't Text Back

You met a girl, ended up with her number, but now you've called or texted her and she hasn't replied. What to do?

When a girl doesn't text back, or when a girl doesn't call back... first, don't panic. It's not the end of the world. It doesn't mean you've lost her for good.

It just means she hasn't gotten back to you yet.

I once texted a girl an icebreaker text the night I met her, and got no reply.

Then I called her a day later, and got no answer. I shot her a text in lieu of a voicemail, and she texted back to apologize and say she hadn't realized it was me.

A few days later, I called her again. Again, no answer. I texted her again, and again she texted back later. But it still didn't go anywhere.

A week after I'd first met her, I called her. Again, no answer. This time, I left a voicemail. She called me back and complained that she had nothing to do that night. So I, ever the good host, invited her over to have dinner and drinks with me at my apartment. A few hours in, I went to use the bathroom and she followed me. I slammed her against the wall of the bathroom and kissed her, then carried her back out and we made love on the sofa.

Persistence. It's the difference between the men who want it and get it, and the men who don't. There were guys I mentored who would have girls disappear and act disinterested, but they'd just persist. Eventually the girls would reappear, agree to meet, and finally end up in bed.

Persistence via text or phone can work wonders... BUT it's crucial to persist in a cool, laid back, socially savvy way. There are myriad wrong ways to persist, and men for some reason are particularly good at finding them. Don't fall into the traps that most men do of getting needy, whiny, complain-y. Don't get angry at women for not replying. Any of those will guarantee you won't get a reply!

Instead, here are some things to keep in mind... so you persist in the kind of intelligent, attractive way most likely to make a girl want to talk to you again:

Don't get mad or accusatory. Yes, it may seem rude that she hasn't replied, but... you're a stranger! She doesn't know you from Jack yet, and doesn't realize what an awesome guy you are. Getting mad is 100% guaranteed to scare her off. Refrain from anything like "I don't understand why you're being so standoffish."

Don't get whiny. Just as bad as mad is sad: whiny, complain-y men are a huge turnoff to every girl out there. "I just want to talk to you. I'm not trying to be too pushy, but blah blah blah." No. You wouldn't care to get something like that from a girl... and a girl will care even less to get something like that from a man.

DO be nonchalant. "Hey Karen, figured I'd drop you a line since we haven't connected in a few weeks. Just got back from the East Coast and starting to delve back into work again... ugh. Hope life's been treating you excellent... let me know what's new with you! - Chase" Treat the situation as if no one is to blame and the two of you are just reconnecting after a little time off, just busy with your own things. If you have some hurt feelings, stifle them. Calls and texts are not the place to air grievances or bandy about bad emotions. You must be a breath of fresh air; a source of escape for her. That's the kind of thing that makes a girl want to pick up the phone and talk to you... because she likely doesn't get it anywhere else in her life. Everyone else puts pressure on her. You just aim to be her release.

DO refrain from being too entertaining. "Just saw the most amazing movie today!" "OMG, think my head is going to explode, you'll never believe what just happened to me...!!!" Anything like that is no good. That kind of stuff is maybe okay three or four texts into a conversation with a girl. But to send that as a cold text, as your text opener, drips of try-hard reaction-seeking. Worse, in my experience, it rarely works. And when it does work, it gets you attention from girls who are curious, not girls who are interested. Stick to normal stuff and you'll do fine.

Finally, don't be afraid to give a girl a little time off if she doesn't reply for a while. My rule of thumb is something like this: she doesn't reply once: give her a day of radio silence. She doesn't reply twice in a row: give her 2 - 3 days of radio silence. She doesn't reply three times in a row: give her a week of radio silence.

Then, if she's still silent, you might try something bolder, depending on the situation. There's no one-shot, surefire way to reengage a girl who isn't responding. It's going to vary by the reason why she doesn't respond in the first place.

If she's too shy, a nice, warm voicemail might do the trick... or tone down your texts if you've come across as to entertaining, gamey, or insincere.

On the other hand, if it feels like too much of a state-shift for her, share some more normal details of your life and ask about hers. Sometimes that's all it takes to help her to see you as more "human"... and get her to respond.

In Summary...

In this chapter, we looked at some of the reasons why a girl may not text back. We discovered it can be because she's too nervous, her mood now is too different from when she met you, your chat with her ended awkwardly or poorly, or she's just not that interested.

We talked a bit about some of the long-term strategic fixes for these. Our top suggestion? Take her number FAST and don't dawdle if the number is your goal. After this, though, we zeroed in on what you can do *now* to troubleshoot girls who aren't texting back *now*.

When she doesn't respond, you want to be persistent. But it's crucial you persist in the right way. The right way means you don't get mad/accusatory or whiny, but you do be nonchalant and you do avoid veering into being an entertainer.

Finally, I gave you my general timeline for following up with a girl who isn't responding to texts: if she doesn't reply once: give her a day of radio silence. If she doesn't reply twice in a row: give her 2 - 3 days of radio silence. If she doesn't reply three times in a row: give her a week of radio silence. And if she still doesn't respond after that, changing up your angle can sometimes work. A warm voicemail, consideration for her, or an invite to a party or art show may be all she needs. It isn't always possible to turn things around when a girl doesn't text back... but sometimes it is.

And if you don't spend too much time with girls from whom you take contact info – say about 3 to 7 minutes – you might just find you substantially raise your phone number conversion rate. Strange as that may seem!

Of course, just because she's agreed to the date doesn't actually mean she'll show up. Thus, in our next chapter, we'll take a close look at what to do when a girl flakes on you.

6

What to Do When She Flakes

Date Plans Dashed

Is there anything more annoying than when a girl you put a lot of time and sweat into texting with flakes on a date with you? You planned everything out to perfection, steeled yourself to ask her, set it all up, and then... she flakes.

She cancels. Or she's a no-show.

No good.

It used to drive me crazy when girls flaked, and I know for a fact it still drives plenty of guys out there crazy.

The good news is it needn't be a dating death sentence. That's because there are plenty of things you can do to prevent flakes before they happen. And even if she does flake, there are still ways to rebound.

We're going to look at both the prevention and the cure.

When a Girl Flakes: It's Not About You

At the end of 2010, I met a girl and set up a date with her. She called me before our date, telling me that her phone's battery was almost out of charge. But we decided where and when we'd meet. I arrived there 10 minutes late; she hadn't arrived yet.

I waited for 10 minutes and didn't see her. I tried to call her, but there wasn't a dial tone; her battery must have died. I waited 10 more minutes. It was now 30 minutes past our meet time, and she wasn't there yet.

So I sent her a text telling her I guess we'd gotten mixed up and that I'd tried calling her but her phone must be dead. Then I turned around, hopped back on the train, and headed back to my part of town. I got some food and went home.

A few hours later, the girl called and very apologetically told me she'd been an hour late because she got lost and couldn't find the place... and the parking had been horrible... and she had to park far away and walk. She said she was very very sorry.

I told her not to worry about it. She said she wanted to make it up to me. I told her she could cook me dinner sometime this week. She said okay.

At the end of the week, she texted me to meet up. I told her to meet me at my subway station, which she did. She pulled up in a car, I got in, and she handed me a box full of chocolates as an apology. And then she noted it was so cold today and asked me if I wanted to just go to my place or drive around. I thought about it for a second and told her we could just go back to my place. So we did.

I had her clothes off within 15 minutes of us reaching my apartment. We stayed in the whole day and had sex four times that afternoon. Later, we went out for food, and she paid for my dinner, again to apologize for missing that original first date.

Were this a few years earlier, I likely would've felt insulted that she flaked and wouldn't have met up with her. Or I might've thought she needed more attraction, so I'd have played games and teased her, which would've cooled things off.

These days, though, when girls flake, I just stay cool. I don't make a big deal out of it. And it's often a happy ending.

Rule #1 to deal with flakes? Don't let it be a big deal. Stay cool when girls flake.

What happens with many guys is they take it personal. If a girl flakes on him, a guy considers it a sign of disrespect. "It's obvious she doesn't respect me, and she doesn't respect my time," he thinks.

You know what I realized? It's not about you. Or at least, it's rarely about you. Most of the time when a girl flakes, it's because something came up, or she misjudged how much time she had to allow to get there, or she started to doubt you'd show up, or the date as arranged was inconvenient or difficult.

It will almost always be something along those lines. It's almost always poor logistics, poor communication, or a date idea she's just not in the mood for. It's almost never a judgment leveled at you yourself.

So don't take it so personal!

Flake Prevention

How do you discourage a girl from flaking? There are a few different ways, and I recommend using all of them (I do):

Be simple and direct in your run-up to the date. The reason I recommend you don't get mired in big phone calls or long text conversations is because unproductive talk time makes things feel overblown; she might start feeling like the date is a big deal, that she really likes you, or that you really like her, and get nervous and jittery and skittish. Believe it or not, longer text or phone conversations do not make her feel happier. Talking to her longer only makes her happier when she talks to you face to face (Vlahovic, Roberts, & Dunbar, 2012). Far better for your texting to be simple and for her to feel like it's casual and easy to meet you – she's a lot more likely to show up.

Pick a date that's easy and convenient. One of the prime reasons you want to simplify your dates is that the easier it is for a girl, the more likely she is to agree. When you try to set up something with too many steps, or something that involves a lot of hard work or activity, you risk mental resistance. That's when she flakes. It might sound fun at first, then she wakes up the day of and thinks "Man, I don't have the energy for laser tag today. Maybe I just won't go." Pick dates that are easy and convenient so as to cut the chances of this happening.

Give a girl a choice of times. One thing I'm big on these days is letting girls choose times. I'll lay out a few days I'm available and suggest we do either a meal or grab a drink. I leave it flexible enough that she can suggest lunch or dinner or drinks, or toss the ball back in my court. When you do it this way, she'll let you know if it's easier for her to do lunch or if she'd rather do drinks, or if any time of day is good for her, and what day is best. Because if you pick a time convenient to her instead of squeezing her into one that doesn't work, you make her much less likely to flake.

Text beforehand. Remember how important it is to text her before the meet? Don't forget it! This is as important to flake prevention as the other bits. As you recall, when you text beforehand, you let her know the date's still on, and you put her at ease. And, if she planned to flake, this prompts her to write back and tell you she won't make it... thereby saving you travel and wait time, and allowing her to save face. You head off the scenario where she fails to tell you, then feels too ashamed about the faux pas to face you again.

These are your primary tools to reduce flakes down to a minimum level in your dating life. Use all these techniques, and you'll slash the likelihood of your dates not showing.

Flake Management

Say you take all your flake prevention measures, and a girl still flakes. Either she's a no-show, or she texts to say she has to cancel. What do you do then?

Just a few simple guidelines in this case. First, don't panic; treat it like it's no big deal. Second, be understanding; tell her it's okay and there's no need to explain if she tries to launch into a long explanation.

Third, don't try to reschedule then and there unless she's adamant. Don't even mention rescheduling. If she brings it up, tell her to just do her thing if she's in a rush, and you'll worry about rescheduling later. You want to communicate confidence that you'll see her again and, once more, that it's no big deal. Aside from this, hastily rescheduled dates are more likely to get moved again. Let her reschedule with you when she's calm, not rushed, and not under an obligation.

However, fourth, do make excuses for girls where necessary. Just like with that girl I had a date with. I texted her that I guess we got mixed up and her phone must have run out of juice. You want to show her you're on her side, that you understand, and give her a possible out. You want to avoid her feeling trapped and like she has to explain herself. Supply her with an explanation, and she'll be far more likely to feel at ease with you, and far more likely to meet you again later.

The basic gist is: it's no big deal.

I've seen guys recommend you call girls out on a flake. I've seen other guys recommend you don't let them off the hook too easily. Still other guys recommend elaborate games to play to re-interest a girl and make her want to see you again. All this, of course, relies on the assumption that the reason she's flaked is that she isn't into you. It's my bet if she's interested enough to say yes to a date in the first place, her interest likely isn't the issue.

More likely, it's that something came up, or she ran late, or she panicked, or got nervous. Or the date you set up was inconvenient for her. Or anything along those lines. Just let her call it off, then reschedule with her a little later, and you solve all these problems.

No ruses, no games to re-spark interest, no radio silence to make her think you're über hard-to-get. Just be chill and reschedule later. No big deal.

In Summary...

I've just armed you with a full set of tools to understand flakes, prevent them, and address them. Before we close the chapter, let's have a quick review.

The first point we covered was that flakes are rarely about you. Often it's something on her end, not yours. She most likely flaked because something came up, she misjudged how much time it would take to get there, she started to doubt you'd show up, or the date as arranged was inconvenient or difficult. So, don't take flakes personal.

The ways to discourage flakes include:

1. Be simple and direct in the run-up to the date
2. Pick a date that's easy and convenient
3. Give her a choice of times
4. Text her before the date

If you do these but she flakes anyway, you should not panic. Treat it like it's no big deal. Do be understanding. Cut off any long explanations. Don't try to reschedule then and there (unless she insists on it). Yet, do make excuses for her if needed.

Great things can happen when you handle a flake well. You may have noticed this in my own flake story, specifically the date following the flake. Handling a girl's flake well tends to make them intrigued... and often ready for rapid intimacy. Why? Because most guys don't know how to handle the situation; they get testy or weak or needy or angry. But you, when you handle a sticky situation like this well... it says more about your strength, confidence, and power as a man than almost anything else you can say or do. And that's the kind of statement about yourself that makes girls want to jump in bed with you fast.

In the next chapter, we'll talk about what to do when your texts just aren't working to get her out on dates.

7

Calls – For When Texts Don't Work

Sometimes You've Got to Change the Medium

I want to talk about a fun little technique. This tech **fractionates**[25] your contact method to get somewhere with girls who don't respond well.

This technique is, simply, switching back and forth between texting and calling.

Now, if you've done things right from the beginning with a girl, you won't usually need to use this. A **great first impression**[26], framing for the date **before you get the number**[27], then solid text

---

[25] GirlsChase.com – "Fractionation Simply Explained"
[26] GirlsChase.com – "A Good First Impression: Making One Every Time"
[27] GirlsChase.com – "How to Get a Phone Number from a Girl Every Time You Ask"

game to set things up... that's usually going to do everything you need it to do.

Usually if you need this technique, it's because you've done something wrong: you made a weak first impression, you didn't make it clear you wanted a date with her, or it could be your texting was weak and/or unfocused.

However, you can still have things unravel sometimes, even if you were "perfect." This is if, say, you do it all right, but when she gets your "Hey, let's get things scheduled" text, it is a bad day for her, and she puts it off. She has just set bad precedent and **anchored bad emotions**[28] to texts from you. Sometimes a girl may get it in her head that "XYZ thing is hard" (like when you fit on her schedule) for reasons she isn't aware of (anchoring). Then, an otherwise promising connection goes cold.

For any such situation, you have one neat tool in your toolbox: just vary the means of correspondence. In this chapter, I'll show you how to do that by switching between texts and phone calls. One note: email and instant messaging are practically the same as texting, so they don't count as switching things up in this context. We're going to be talking "text-based" vs. "voice-based" here.

---

[28] GirlsChase.com – "How to Use Anchoring to Mesmerize Women"

Objections to Text/Call Splitting

There are three primary objections to text/call splitting, so let's address those first.

1. If she doesn't respond to my texts, why bother?
2. Isn't making a phone call intrusive?
3. Isn't using phone calls dated/outmoded in today's day and age?

We'll discuss.

#1: Why Bother?

This objection is no different from anything else with meeting women: "**Cold approach is hard**[29]. Why bother?" "**Men have to lead**[30]. Why can't I wait for girls to lead?" "All this 'learn game[31]' stuff is a lot of work. Why not **just be myself**[32] instead?" The answer here is the same: because it works.

Not everyone wants to do everything, and that I understand. But if you're a guy who won't text/call split because he doesn't want to, then complains that women don't text him back... well, that's just silly.

Some guys view such techniques (where you continue to follow up with a girl who isn't bursting at the seams for you) as chase-y.

[29] GirlsChase.com – "Why Cold Approach Works Better Than Anything Else"
[30] GirlsChase.com – "The Real Reason Many Men Can't Get a Girl"
[31] GirlsChase.com – "Do You Really Need to Learn Game to Get Girls?"
[32] GirlsChase.com – "Just Be Yourself: The Worst Dating Advice Known to Man"

Sure, they are... if you're doing them wrong, but you can say that of anything.

Imagine this: a busy, important man meets a beautiful girl. He texts her to meet up several times, but it doesn't pan out. Meantime, he's going on dates with other girls, too.

One day on his way to the gym, he takes out his phone and calls this girl. She answers, they chat, he sets up a date with her before the call ends, and then he hangs up and goes on about his day.

Chasing? No.

This is how you'll be using this technique.

#2: Isn't Making a Phone Call Intrusive?

Not as intrusive as what you'll be doing to her in the bedroom. ;)

To a certain extent, you want to be considerate of a girl's time and not put too much pressure on her early on (before you're lovers). At least this is how you want to kick things off. I'll tell you a secret, though... not all women are created equal.

Some women desire a man who'll leave a minimal footprint on their lives – one who'll make things easy and low pressure for them, and take up little of their time. Other women desire a man who's going to impose himself on them in attractive and savvy ways. They desire a man who will force them to pay attention to him.

The nice thing about the text/call split technique is that it starts out: "I'll be cool and we'll do this in an unimposing way." Then, if she does not respond to that approach, it switches to: "Hey, I'm important, so let's set this up."

Dating itself is an intrusive process. You intrude on her time, intrude on her thoughts and dreams, and at last intrude into her body. If you're (overly – a little is good) worried about being "too intrusive" with a girl you want to copulate with... well, maybe it's time for a little **asshole training**[33].

Also, keep in mind, some girls actually prefer phone calls over text (Reid & Reid, 2004; Rettie, 2007). By starting with text, then moving to phone if it isn't working, you enable yourself to cover both groups.

#3: Aren't Phone Calls So 20th Century?

There's also this objection that asks: "Who makes a phone call anymore?" The answer, of course, is "busy people." Phone calls simply are just the best communication medium for certain kinds of talk (LaBowe, 2011).

When you try to set something up over text, and it isn't working, the only people who keep texting are students with too much time on their hands and other people who don't have too many things to do.

That doesn't mean YOU have to only text girls in college or girls with too much time on their hands. They understand and appreciate a good phone call from a busy man as much as anyone else.

---

[33] GirlsChase.com – "How to Be an Asshole – and Become Adored by Women"

The busy guy just calls. Instead of 100 text messages and half a day of typing and waiting, he can accomplish everything with a 2-minute phone call.

If you are successful with women, you will be busy. And the kind of men women find attractive are those who are busy. One of the things you'll notice is that the busier you get, the easier dating gets, and it's not a coincidence. Busyness works as a kind of implicit **preselection**[34]. If it's obvious you don't have a huge amount of time for her (without you being "fake busy"), that says good things about you. It says you live in **abundance**[35] and have **things that are important to you**[36] in your life.

Another alternative to the text/call split is the "ball in your court" text (we'll talk about it in two chapters). You can use one of these techniques, or both of them. If you've already done a few phone calls, and she still won't come out, you will actually want to do a "ball in your court call" call instead of text... but we'll talk about that later.

One other group of people who prefer phone calls to texts are lonely people (Reid & Reid, 2007). You'll find some girls may be slow to respond or non-responsive over text, but very responsive over phone – especially if they are sad, lonely, or depressed. Phone is simply a more personal medium, and one that's better for people who desire a more personal touch.

Phone calls are as good now as they always have been IF your phone game is good (same IF as it's always been). Like anything,

---

[34] GirlsChase.com – "How Preselection Works to Get You Girls"
[35] GirlsChase.com – "Absolute Abundance"
[36] GirlsChase.com – "The Purpose of Life from a Practical Point of View"

this is a skill you have to train, and it takes a little time. So if you aren't used to talking on the phone, it can feel like phone calls aren't working that great for you, because they aren't yet.

If that's the case for you, make sure to check out these GirlsChase.com articles:

- "Talking vs. Texting & Related Tips" (note: my stance on text-dates has changed)
- "Tactics Tuesdays: Making the First Phone Call to a Girl"
- "Call Girls to Success: Phone Secrets Part II"

How to Call/Text Split

These days, I suggest you usually start with texts. But not always. We'll cover situations where you want to lead with phone calls a little later in this chapter. However, usually you will lead with texting. That's because it's easy, low pressure, and the learning curve's shorter than phone calls.

You only need to be good at basic logistics-handling texts to get dates with text game, provided of course you're doing everything else right before you get the phone number. So it cuts down on the level of skill you need to get dates, which is what long-distance correspondence is all about: **get her out in person with you.**

You should usually only use phone calls these days when one or more of the following is true: (a) you sent her icebreaker and follow-up texts, and she didn't respond; (b) you tried to set up a date(s) via text, and she flaked or didn't respond; (c) she has continually dodged date requests or is hard to pin down.

In each of these cases, the phone call ups the ante. Continuing to text when she's evasive positions you as the chaser. She's given you little or nothing, yet you keep tossing her bones. Or, at this point, you can use the ball-in-your-court text to say "Okay, well, when you're ready, you text me." But that takes it out of your hands. She may call back, she may not.

My general recommendation on when to use text/call splits vs. the ball-in-your-court text is: if you're "meh" about the girl, throw the ball in her court; if you'd really like to see the girl, text/call split. If you're good at phone game, you'll tend to find phone calls have a better percentage than ball-in-her-court texts. Calls are also a heck of a lot more time efficient.

That means, if you don't have a lot of time (say, you'll leave town soon), OR you just want to get this girl ASAP (if she'll be off the market soon... or if you just really like her), there's no point pretending you don't care – and bouncing her the "it's in your court" text – when you do care. You also don't need to wait 2 weeks for her to decide she wants to date you, either.

If you want her – and texts aren't working – then call her. Here's how you do that, in four steps.

Step #1: Good Text/Impression Game

How likely she is to answer your phone call is directly tied to how solid your text message game is, and how good a first impression you made. If these sucked, she'll have bad emotions anchored to your name on the screen, and she'll be less likely to answer. If your text game was good and your first impression was good, she's going to tend to want to answer your call. That's because she'll see you as a source of good emotions.

Women are constantly in search of good emotions. If they view you as someone who can provide these, they will welcome you into their lives. That means: don't just be lazy with your texts and assume you'll call her if it doesn't work out. You still need good text game. Without that, she's less likely to answer your call.

Step #2: Time It Properly

Especially if you're new, it's important to give her enough time to respond to texts.

Some girls take hours to get back to you; some can take a day. This doesn't necessarily mean they aren't interested; although, if she doesn't respond in 3 or 4 hours, you probably have work to do once she's on the date. It can simply mean a girl's busy, or keeps her phone on silent, or doesn't check messages a whole lot. Believe it or not, there are girls out there who don't check their messages a whole lot... mostly **professional women**[37] or others with a lot going on (whose lives don't revolve around InstaSnapBookTwitter).

So don't fall into the trap where you text a girl, she doesn't respond right away, and then 90 minutes later you're calling her. It

---

[37] GirlsChase.com – "What's Different When Picking Up Professional Women?"

looks scared and needy, like you sat around staring at your phone, and called when you didn't hear back.

Instead, a typical progression might look something like this:

1. Meet the girl
2. [3 hours later] Ice-breaker text
3. [next day] Follow-up plus date-ask
4. [IF says no / dodges – 2 days later] Phone call with date-ask
5. [IF no date / dodges – 3 days later] Text invite to something different
6. [IF no date / dodges – 2 days later] Bonding phone call with no date-ask
7. [3 days later] Phone call with date-ask
8. [IF says no / dodges – 3 days later] Text invite to something different
9. [IF says no / dodges – that night] Ball-in-your-court phone call

That's five date invites in a two-week period without feeling rushed, crammed-in, or try-hard. That's pretty good. It's good because it filters for as many variables as possible: maybe she doesn't want a date one day you ask, but she does on another; maybe she doesn't like one of your date ideas, so you cycle through others; maybe she doesn't like one medium (texts), but is happy to get a phone call.

When you switch tactics up, you give yourself room to find an angle that works for a girl where previous angles did not.

Step #3: Keep It Fresh

It's important to hit the right note of fresh + familiar. You want to talk about **some topics you've previously covered**[38]... while at the

---

[38] GirlsChase.com – "Secrets to Getting Girls: Nicknames and Callback"

same time introducing new information, ideas, and stimuli. For instance, you never want to propose the same date idea twice in a row. Don't be the guy who invites her to coffee on Monday, gets a "Not right now, thanks," then texts her again inviting her to coffee on Thursday... then texts her again on Sunday to invite her to coffee again.

Instead, be the guy who invites her to coffee on Monday, then invites her to an art gallery opening on Thursday. And if she declines both of those, invites her to go hiking with him on Sunday. Vary it up. That's for two reasons: it gives you the chance to strike on something she'll say "yes" to, and it makes you more **intriguing**[39]: "What's Scott going to propose this time?"

For the phone calls, follow the phone call guide and make sure you have a recent short story prepped to go. You won't always need it, but it's handy to have sitting there at-the-ready. You can launch into your story to warm the conversation up if she doesn't jump into the chat right away.

Step #4: Texts for Logistics, Phone Calls for Bonding

Keep this rule in mind: text messages are for logistics, phone calls are for bonding.

If you had a quick interaction when you first met her (e.g., a 2-minute number close)... or you didn't have the smoothest interaction

---

[39] GirlsChase.com – "Be Intriguing. Be Memorable."

and then kind of fumbled the follow-up over text... you might need to do a little bonding before she feels comfortable enough to meet you. That's where phone calls come in.

Don't use texts to try to build connections, due to the lack of context. You can joke around on texts, and you can set up logistics, but they aren't ideal for much else. Your sexy bedroom voice plus 10 minutes talking to her on the phone can be enough to swing a lot of girls from "on the fence about you" to "fully onboard."

The greater context of phone calls also makes them more resistant to negative anchoring. For example, if she starts associating bad emotions with your texts ("He's too pushy" or "His texts are boring" or "He always texts me at inconvenient times"), it's easy for her to anchor these emotions to you and not want to answer. However, with phone calls, especially if you're good at phone game, it's easy to inject energy, enthusiasm, and variety. These make it easier for you to anchor strong positive emotions... insomuch that even if she declines a few dates, or if you don't always call at convenient times, you still provide energy that makes her want to answer your call.

If she seems uncertain about you over text, or she's being dodgy, call her. It ups the ante ("Okay, let's get serious about this") and reassures (and re-attracts) her in ways texts can't.

Call/Text Splitting Caveats

There are some caveats to what we've laid out in this article, too. These are that you must call FIRST if you're time-pressed or if she's clearly hot for you, and that once you've introduced calling, any ball-in-your-court communication must be over a call, not text. Here's what these two caveats mean.

When to Call First

The normal rule is: lead with texts, follow (if needed) with phone calls. However, sometimes you don't have time for texting and waiting, texting and waiting.

When you're just in town for a few days, for instance, texting can murder your odds to see a girl again. Even if she wants to meet you, by the time you get it all scheduled, you may already be on your train or flight out of there.

In this case, even if leading with a phone call perhaps isn't the social norm per se, still do it. If your phone game is good, it won't matter, because as soon as she's on the phone, she'll be thrilled to talk to you again.

Additionally, sometimes you meet a girl and you can tell she's super excited to meet up with you again. When this is the case, it's often better to lead with calls over texts.

Leading with calls brings her back to a richer communication channel, which is what she wants. Ideally, she wants to be with you, not be chatting with you at a distance. Calls are much closer to actually being with you than texts are. So you can call, remind her what she's so excited about, and get her to meet up, hopefully pronto.

You may run into the scenario where a girl is piping hot for you in-person, then you start to text her and she grows cold. And then you call her again, and she's hot again. What's happening here is the texting is a let-down for her. She doesn't want to interact with words on a screen that represent you. She wants to interact with you yourself. So, when you have girls who clearly really like you, you may find you're better off with phone calls rather than texts.

What if the first phone call doesn't get you a date? No problem; just use text/call splitting, and continue to switch it up.

What Medium to Use With Ball-in-Her-Court Messages

Usually the ball-in-her-court message is done via text. However, if you introduce phone calls, you need to do this via phone, not text. The reason why is because phone calls are a more serious, more "real" medium than text.

If you're already chatting to her via phone call and you give her a very "real" message like "When you've got time and want to grab a drink, drop me a line and let me know" over text, it comes across as a little cowardly. *Oh, so he can talk to me over phone about ABC and DEF, but he can't tell me I'm avoiding him and ask me to let him know when I'm ready over the phone? Scaredy cat!*

Do not ask her out and also give her a ball-in-her-court message in the same call; it sounds spiteful.

Don't do this:

> **You:** ... blah blah blah. So anyway, we should grab one of those mojitos you keep talking about – want to do that this week?

> **Her:** You know, this week's actually really busy for me. I don't think I can.

> **You:** Okay. Well, it seems like you're always pretty busy lately. Tell you what, I'm not so good at the whole chasing-you-around thing, so why don't we leave it off for a while, and then when you've got some time you can drop me a line and let me know when you want to meet up?

Feels like you're being kind of whiney or bitter here, doesn't it? That's because you're immediately following the rejection up with the ball-in-your-court message. This is different in text. Since because a text message is much less personal, everything feels less *serious*. Her declining your date isn't that big of a deal, just like you throwing the ball in her court isn't one either. So you can follow up a rejected date request with a ball-in-her-court message. It doesn't feel like you're saying this just because your feelings are hurt.

However, for the phone call ball-in-her-court, you need to do things differently. So, instead, ask her out via text, and if she dodges/rejects, call her that night and have a short (2 or 3 minute) call... then ball-in-her-court her.

That looks like this:

[2 to 3 minutes of small talk/chit-chat]

> **You:** Yeah, so anyway, seems like you're super busy/tough to meet up with!

> **Her:** Yeah, you know, I work long hours, and this project I'm on right now is sucking up ALL my free time.

> **You:** I completely understand. I had a project like that about 4 months ago. It was fun, but my social life just vanished. Hey, so, I don't want to keep calling you and texting you and distracting you when you're so busy, and I'm also terrible at the whole chasing thing, as you can probably tell. [pause; let her laugh] So I'll quit bugging you for now, but I'd really like to meet up with you at some point and quit being strangers over a phone line. Tell you what, when you get some free time, shoot me a text or give me a call and let's meet up, that work?

Then say your goodbyes and get off the phone.

Note the difference in tone and message structure from the ball-in-your-court text message. It's much more conversational here, and you put more time in to communicate "I get where you're coming from, and I understand." That's because the phone is a richer medium, and it's important you make it clear you're not saying this because you're smarting.

Also, the reason you call her that night boils down to a basic premise of **operant conditioning**[40]. That is, positive punishment

---

[40] GirlsChase.com – "Operant Conditioning in Your Romantic Relationships"

(removing something she enjoys) works best when it closely follows the bad behavior it punishes.

In this case, her brushing aside yet another date request is the bad behavior. The positive punishment is that now you're going to wait for her to contact you. And you aren't going to call her and provide good feelings, happiness, and excitement anymore.

If you do this 2 or 3 days after the rejection, or even the next day, the feeling has waned, and she won't tie the punishment to the behavior. That makes her less likely to think "Oops – I caused this; I did something wrong... I'd better fix it if I want the good feelings back." Instead, she's more likely to think "Hmm, I guess he's just giving up," or "Maybe he found someone else; I should probably move on, too."

If you need to use the ball-in-your-court call, time is of the essence.

In Summary...

Let's sum this chapter up.

Some of the reasons you might want/need to use this technique: you made a weak first impression, you didn't make it clear you wanted a date with her, your texting was weak and/or unfocused, your texting accidentally got negatively anchored for her, or she just doesn't like texting that much.

The big three objections to text/call splitting are:

1. If she doesn't respond to my texts, why bother?
2. Isn't making a phone call intrusive?
3. Isn't using phone calls dated/outmoded in today's day and age?

The responses are:

1. It's not chasing; if you actually want to meet her/get laid, you'll bother ;)
2. Phone calls *are* more intrusive than text. Sex is even more intrusive, though
3. Phone calls still work **awesome** (IF you develop good phone game. Big IF)

You should usually just use phone calls when you sent her ice-breaker and follow-up texts but she didn't respond, or you tried to set up a date(s) via text but she flaked or didn't respond, or she's continually dodging date requests or is hard to pin down. In each of these cases, the phone call (being a higher context medium) serves to up the ante.

When deciding whether to call/text split or just throw the ball in her court over text without ever giving her a call, my recommendation is this: if you're "meh" about the girl, throw the ball in her court... but if you'd really like to see the girl, text/call split.

Steps for using call/text splitting to good effect:

1. Make a good first impression and text her well before you ever call her
2. Use proper timing in spacing out and planning texts and phone calls
3. Keep your conversations and date suggestions fresh
4. Texts are for logistics, calls are for bonding

And the two caveats to call/text splitting: call FIRST if you're time-pressed *or* if she's clearly hot for you. And if you introduce calling, any ball-in-your-court communication has to be over a phone call, not text.

Remember, the phone-call version of ball-in-your-court has several rules the text-only version does not. These include:

1. Make the call after she brushes off a text-based date invite
2. Call her the same day she rejects the invitation
3. 2 to 3 minutes of small talk, then ball-in-your-court message
4. Make it clear you understand where she's coming from
5. Leave it very open for her to contact you when she's ready

Lots of rules, details, and nuance here, I realize; many of these things are more minor details, however. If you want the easy quick-start guide to call/text splitting, here it is:

Switch it up between date requests over text versus chatting and date requests over the phone.

If you're brand-spanking new to all this, I wouldn't worry about too many more of the details than this. Once you're more comfortable with text/call splitting, then come back to this chapter.

At that point, observe which rules you've already begun to follow instinctively. Then add in the other rules you aren't using yet that will most immediately help you out.

In the next chapter, we'll talk about how to pick things up again with a girl you haven't talked to in a while. And in the chapter after that, we'll take a detailed look at that ball-in-her-court communication.

8

Texting When It's Been a While

Haven't Seen You in Some Time

Sometimes you might have a situation where you lose touch with the girl for a while. Whether it's because it didn't go anywhere or you just forgot, you quit texting her. And she quits texting you.

Then one day you stumble across her number again or recall her, and you think "Man, that girl was cute. I'd like to see her again." But it's been so long and she's likely moved on. How do you get back in touch?

The way you do this is with what I call the "check-in" text. It's a way to pick up with a girl you've lost touch with. And you do it in a nice, natural way.

She Doesn't Know Where You've Gone

You don't know where she is or what she's up to. But by the same token, she doesn't know this about you, either. She doesn't know why you haven't been in contact. She has no idea why the texts from you stopped.

It could be you just gave up your efforts to get her. It could be because you got busy. It could be you were on travel, or got a girlfriend, or got engaged. There's no way for her to know.

She's also unlikely to recall the tone when you quit texting her. She won't remember if she was short with you. She won't remember if you chased a little too hard. Unless you were desperate in your texts, if some time has gone by, she'll have forgotten. It's the old "time heals all wounds" cliché, but here it's true. If things didn't go perfectly before, give her some time to reset, and try again.

Remember, she's a girl. She's busy. She likely texts a LOT of people. Even if you made an impression before, if you drop off her radar, you get a reset. She does too much texting to remember the details of who is what to her for long.

Sure, she might skim through her past texts with you and read what you wrote before. But a lot of girls won't bother. If they get a text they like from you now, they won't care. Only the obsessive types go back and reread messages. The rest squint, say "Oh yeah, that guy," and if they like the message, they want to meet.

So there are two key factors here: she doesn't know why you stopped texting, and she doesn't recall the dynamic exactly.

What's a situation like this do for you? Simple: it lets you **reframe**[41] your disappearance any way you want to.

The Standard Check-In Text

The standard check-in text contains these five elements:

1.   Greeting and her name
2.   Apologies for why you've been quiet
3.   Explanation that you've been busy
4.   Ask her how she is
5.   Ask her out and request her schedule

The **greeting and name** we've already covered in the chapter on how to text a girl. So let's talk about the other four.

Apologies: but Chase, isn't it bad to apologize, you ask? Well, yes, usually. But in this case, you are apologizing for you having marginalized and forgotten her. The thing you "did wrong" makes you high status and important, yet her low status and unimportant. She sat around and waited for you, and you forgot her. And now you want to make it up to her. It doesn't matter if this isn't 100% the case. It doesn't matter if she started to ignore you. All that matters is that you frame it this way. If you do, most of the girls you text will treat it like it is actually the case. Funny, right?

---

[41] GirlsChase.com – "Frame Control Examples: Out-Frame Anyone"

You've been busy: here, you just want to say you've been busy. You can mention the "why" if you like, but it isn't necessary. You just want to give her an understandable reason for your absence. This makes your check-in text congruent... you were busy, and now things have cleared up (and you have time for her). This is the "piece of new information" part of a new text conversation.

Ask how she is: as you recall, "consideration" is one of four elements to include in a new cold text. Here you ask how she is to show consideration... and also because it's just a normal thing for people to do who haven't spoken in a while. This way, if she has anything important she needs to update you on, you've given her a social window to do so.

Ask her out and request her schedule: and lastly, you want to get right to the point: ask her for her schedule. This way she doesn't have to wonder what the message is about. She doesn't need to ask herself what you're after. It's right there in the text. "Oh, okay – he wants to grab drinks and catch up."

Here's an example of what these elements look like all put together:

> Hey Gina! Sorry I've been radio silent these past 6 weeks; I wasn't ignoring you, I just got so slammed with my projects that everything outside of work got pigeonholed until life returned to sanity again. Anyway, things have cleared up a bit. How've you been? Let me know your schedule over the next week or two, and let's plan to meet up and catch up on things.

Pretty straightforward, right? Here's another one:

> Becky, hey! Sorry to drop off the map, I got super busy with work & got on this intense schedule at the gym and just became a total hermit. Argh. Anyway, I am returning to normal socialization again! How're things with you? How'd the new job search go? We should grab a bite or drink and catch up – let me know when you're free!

It's so simple, so nice, and so friendly it's hard for her not to respond. Because you apologize for ignoring her, it feels impolite for her to not say anything back. Of course, when she responds, she accepts your frame that you were the ignorer and she the ignored. See how that works?

Odds are you lost contact because she was being noncommittal. But I'll tell you: this text gets girls to forget how flighty they were with you 9 times out of 10. Those formerly flighty girls will say "Oh, I must've liked this guy" and agree to meet up. Or even if they remember you, they get that shift in psychology and say "You know what, let me give this guy a shot."

Non-Standard Check-In Texts

The standard check-in text will be your text reset bread and butter. It's what you'll use most of the time, with most girls. But what do you do in more extreme situations? A member of the Girls Chase forums asks:

> To boil it down to brass tacks, what's needed is a way to generate interest from a woman we have only met once, a year to 18 months ago; number close, good chemistry but no date or same night lay. They may well be married and pregnant by now. But they might also still be free & easy and living nearby and would benefit from spending time with us and our recently-realigned perspectives on how to give her what she wants & needs via fun & frolicsome encounters. So what's needed is a "non-weird-blast-from-the-past-icebreaker" in SMS Format. Maybe a bit too "magic bullet" to actually be able to realize, but even some half-baked ideas would be fun!

So, what do you do in these more extreme situations... where you hardly know the girl or it's been far too long since you talked to them? Well, you need something a bit more extreme than the standard check-in text. You also need a good reason why you've decided to write her after a year or more of silence. As it turns out, I have just the thing. Two just-the-things, as a matter of fact.

Option #1: Clearing Out My Phone

Your first option is to go through your phone and clear out old phone numbers that didn't pan out. As you delete old numbers, look for girls you'd like to take one more shot with. When you find them, text them this:

> Gina, how ARE you? It's Chase! I'm sorry I haven't talked to you in forever... I just got caught up with things, and totally didn't get in touch. My bad. Listen, I was going through deleting old numbers, and wanted to touch bases again and see what's up. Are you still in town? Want to grab a coffee sometime?

You'll get some hilarious responses back to this. Some of these girls will only very vaguely remember you (or they won't remember you at all)... and they just assume from the tone of the text that the two of you must have been close... somehow.

They'll meet up with you, both intrigued and skeptical, and they'll want to remember how you met. Usually you want to be semi-vague here. Don't try to completely jog their memories. The past isn't important. Just treat them like an old friend, be sorry that you haven't followed up, and get on with things.

You can actually get a nice boost sometimes with these girls. They'll feel like because they've known you for so long, they don't have to be as on-guard with you as they are with most men. And you still get the benefit of being on their romantic and sexual radar screens... unlike most of the men they've known a long time and have long since plunked into the friend zone.

You're the long-lost guy they never got with, but who's stepped back into their lives. It's a fine place to be.

Option #2: Leaving Town

If you plan to leave the city (or country), you can pick numbers out of your phone and text this:

> Gina, hey, it's Chase! I know I haven't been in touch lately, even though I said I would be... I'm sorry, and that's on me. I got caught up with some things before, and never ended up following up with you way back when. Anyway, I'm going through and letting everyone know that I'm moving to Nantucket next Thursday. I don't know what you're doing, but if you'd like to grab a hot chocolate or an ice cream before I'm out of here, I'd love to see you one last time.... Shall we do that?

In my experience, this message gets you a greater response rate than Option #1... that is, she's more likely to respond. However, the rate she comes out on a date is lower than with the first option. My guess is the first is more romantic; this one's more "I'm leaving town; last chance to hook up." She'll only take it if she's in the mood for a no-strings "it doesn't count" hookup with a guy who'll soon be gone.

But if you've got 10 or 20 numbers that never went anywhere and you're on your way out, there's no reason not to use it. You might surprise yourself with what you get from it.

Aren't These Texts Too Long?

If you're familiar with my material, you're likely familiar with the **Law of Least Effort**[42]. And if that's the case, you might wonder: don't these long texts violate the LLE? Or, even if you have no idea what the Law of Least Effort is, maybe you'll just say "That is one long-ass text. Who even texts like that?"

The Law of Least Effort just says the most socially powerful man is the one who gets the greatest results for the least amount of effort. If you can send one text, and do in one text what it takes most guys multiple texts and hours of texting and waiting to do, that's lower effort.

And when it's been a while, you need a long text like this to get your message through. If you think you're going to text her "Hey Gina, what's going on? Sorry I've been busy. What's up with you?" and get into a text conversation, it won't happen. She doesn't remember you, or you haven't chatted with her, so you're irrelevant.

You need the long text format to get enough information in that her mental process goes: "Who is this guy?" → "Oh, right, I remember him. Why is he texting me?" →"Oh, I see, he was busy. But now he's free. Hmm." →"Oh, he wants to meet up with me. Busy guy has time for me now, huh?"

You want to roll from one of those emotions to the next before they have time to cement. You don't want the message to end with her thinking "Who is this guy?" because when your next message comes, you're already a question mark. You don't want it to end on

---

[42] GirlsChase.com – "The Law of Least Effort"

"Why is he texting me?" because now you have to fight her skepticism.

The long text with everything in it violates social convention somewhat. Yet it's so exuberant and so sincere that it doesn't matter. Ever get an excited, happy, but also apologetic long text from a girl? I have, plenty of times, and you never care that it's long. You just catch the emotions she's sending over – and those emotions feel good.

In Summary...

We've just armed you with a few texts to send to pick things up with girls you haven't talked to in a while.

We've covered the five elements a check-in text must contain:

1. Greeting and her name
2. Apologies for why you've been quiet
3. Explanation that you've been busy
4. Ask her how she is
5. Ask her out and request her schedule

And we've given you examples of how to write a standard check-in text, plus examples for two more texts: the "clearing out my phone" text and the "leaving town" text.

Those are texts you can use to reconnect with girls you haven't talked to in forever... sometimes even years. They're lower percentage (the more time that passes, the less likely you are to hear back). But if you have a bunch of numbers, you can send the message out and often get a text or two (or sometimes more) back.

The next chapter looks at how to throw the ball into a girl's court. You can do this any time, with girls you meet in bars, at parties, or via social circle. However, we'll focus particularly on how to do this over text message. How do you tell her you're done chasing her and "program" her to ask you out for a date later?

9

When to Throw the Ball in Her Court

A Line You Learn to Love

"The ball's in your court."

You either love to utter that line, or you never utter it.

It's a liberating line when you use it right. Some girl you think likes you, or you think might like you, but who is being coy or difficult about coming out... you're just going to fire that text off to her, and forget about her.

Or a girl you met somewhere social, but she won't accompany you: "Come find me later." Maybe she will, maybe she won't. It can be hard to say things like this, and even harder to stick to them when you're new and **chasing girls**[43] is second nature. Even if you

---

[43] GirlsChase.com — "Why Chasing Women Doesn't Work and Why Persistence Does"

manage to tell a girl the ball's in her court, you may find yourself texting her the next day anyway... or the day after.

And the opposite is sometimes true. You might find you shove girls off your plate too quickly and too often. This can happen if you don't want to deal with the sometimes-stressful dance of dating. Perhaps that girl you told to get in touch with you later, who never did, would've gotten together with you... had you persisted just a little bit harder in person or over text.

Where to persist versus when to toss the ball in her court is a dicey call sometimes... yet it may determine the difference between you chasing after her and still not getting her... versus you flipping the script on her and getting her to chase you.

Throwing the Ball to Her

First, the technique. How's this done, exactly? Well, what you'll look for before you turn the ball over to the girl are several signs:

1. You've persisted and tried to get compliance or a date from her, but she's resisted or flaked again and again
2. You've determined her resistance or flakiness isn't from you trying to shoehorn her into anything uncomfortable
3. You've made multiple different overtures, and none of them have worked

In other words, it isn't just that you've said "Hey, let's go sit down!" six times and she's resisted. Instead, you've tried "Hey, let's go sit" and "Let's hit the patio and get some fresh air" and "We ought to get out of here and go somewhere more fun," and none of them worked.

And it isn't just that you've invited her to coffee at midday. But instead, you've tried inviting her out to get drinks at night, too. And you've asked her to take a walk by the beach with you when the other offers didn't work.

Because if you just go for one sort of invitation like a stubborn bull, you can miss that you're getting a "no" because she doesn't like the thing you're inviting her to do... not because she doesn't like you.

Not everyone likes coffee... or maybe she doesn't want to sit. Maybe she wants some guy who's just going to get her out of there, and the idea a long seduction when what she wants is sex right now is a buzz kill.

So, you change up your offers. You throw a few other things out there. You feel her out, and see what sticks.

And if nothing sticks, then you can throw the ball in her court.

That looks like this:

> **Her:** ... and so I moved to Los Angeles.
>
> **You:** That's for sure a unique journey. [pause] Hey, let's grab a seat over there.
>
> **Her:** Nah... I'm good over here.
>
> **You:** We'll be much more comfortable sitting down.
>
> **Her:** I was sitting all day; I'd rather stand.

You: All right. Tell you what then, let's mosey on out to the patio and get a little fresh air in that case. That way you can stay upright and we can change scenery.

Her: I'm okay here I think.

You: Yeah? Well, you want to just get out of here? This place is a little dull and you don't exactly seem riveted. We can find somewhere more fun to head to.

Her: I'll just stay here for now.

You: Okay. Well, I need a little more stimulation than propping up lazy against a bar, so I'm going to go shuffle around a bit. But come find me later when you're feeling more active.

Her: Okay.

This is a "going nowhere fast" interaction where you start smooth and get more and more blunt... because screw it, it's not going anywhere, so might as well toss something out there and see if she bites.

The "let's get out of here" line toward the end is a low-percentage shot that doesn't hurt you if it's well worded. She was already turning you down like nobody's business, and it looked like nothing would come of it... so it's worth a shot just because sometimes you will get a *shrug* "Okay, why not" response to this... and then somehow you've snatched victory out of the jaws of defeat.

In any event, in the above scenario, when you still get a "no" to your final offer, you deliver your **parting shot**[44]. You tell her the ball's in her court. And then you leave.

Maybe she finds you again later; maybe she doesn't. But either way, you won't worry about it, because you'll busy yourself to meet other girls who aren't her.

When You're Too Afraid to Do It

Something that can happen when you're new is you struggle to find the courage to tell her the ball's in her court. There's no way around this other than to just forge ahead through it the first couple of times.

You'll tell her "Okay – ball's in your court" a little awkwardly after she's shut down your efforts to get anywhere with her. Then you'll slink off in defeat. She likely won't follow up. But that's okay. The important thing is to build the capability here.

Once you've done this a few times, you'll stop stressing out about it. It'll just be a normal thing you say and do at that stage in the interaction. Then, once it ceases being something you get a little weird about, that's when you'll start having girls follow up with you again.

Here's an example of when you'd send a ball's-in-your-court text: you text her to meet up with you for coffee Tuesday evening. She flakes on that date the night before; something came up. You reschedule to hit the park with her Saturday afternoon. She flakes

---

[44] GirlsChase.com – "The Parting Shot"

the day of; she feels a little under the weather. You reschedule again – hookah bar Monday. She flakes a third time, apologetically.

You send her a ball's-in-your-court text:

> "Haha, all right. Well, I know you're super busy and I'm not really good at doing the whole chase-you-down thing. So you're in charge of planning the next meet, whenever your schedule permits – just let me know a little ahead of time."

or

> "Hey, no worries. I think that's 3 meets I've planned you've had to take a rain check on, so planning for the next attempt is on you! You're the busy one, so I'm leaving that ball in your court. Just let me know when and where once your schedule allows."

You've got to be able to drop the parting shot like this and **walk away**[45]. You can't go text her the next day and try to schedule another date after a ball's-in-your-court text. That reveals your hand (i.e., that you're not a guy with a lot of options... you're a guy without them. **Girls like their guys to have options**[46]).

So if you're going to tell her the ball's in her court, make sure you mean it, and don't go back on your word.

Same with interacting in person. Don't tell her "Come find me later" and then you find her later yourself anyway. (Exception: if you're at a bar or party and everyone's been drinking, and it's much later in the night. Then it can be fine, because you're both a little

---

[45] GirlsChase.com – "I Don't Chase 'Em, I Replace 'Em"
[46] GirlsChase.com – "How Preselection Works to Get You Girls"

hazy and no one remembers exactly who said what... just that the two of you got along well earlier and meant to reconnect later.)

In essence, if you tell her to do something, you're usually just going to have to wait for her to do it.

When You're Using It Too Liberally

The danger of this technique, once you've got it down, is that you grow too comfortable with it.

Once you know how to do it, it becomes easy to just throw out a "Okay, well, it's too early in the night for me to get rooted into one spot; come find me later!" and get moving again at the first sign of resistance... or tell a girl the ball's in her court after she's flaked on you for a date only once or twice.

If you do this, though, you will leave plenty of girls to scratch their heads and wonder what they did or said to make you take off.

Something to keep in mind: women carefully evaluate your exits.

They know very well – intuitively – if your exit was justified, because you tried everything possible to get them to invest in as smooth a way as possible. And when it became clear they wouldn't invest, you bowed out... or your exit was too quick, too abrupt, too sudden, or too awkward. You didn't feel out if they were into you or just put up token resistance to further investment in you (a girl can't look too eager, now).

Men eject too soon from interactions with women all the time to preserve their egos. It's quite common. It's not just men learning to date. It's all kinds of guys. They hit a rough patch in the conversation, get a little bit of declined compliance, or an awkward pause? They're outta there. They just hit the eject button and bail.

This is every bit as uncomfortable for the girl as it is for the guy, because she knows there isn't a good reason for it. He just does it out of fear (of negative social repercussions)... or because he doesn't know what else to do (which can be kind of cute when you're younger – **younger women are attracted to male shame**[47] – but it still doesn't advance the interaction any further).

When you catch yourself throwing out parting shots too liberally... and you'll be able to tell; it feels awkward when you leave, like it's too early and you've jumped the gun too much... the solution for this is simple enough:

Make yourself make at least one more invitation or compliance request of a different angle than you've made. She doesn't want to walk over to the café across the street with you? No worries, let's just head over to the mall, then. She flaked on the ice skating date you invited her to? No problem, propose she meet you for pizza and beer. Try at least one alternate option for your invitations/compliance requests.

Three seems to be the sweet spot for variety. If she's flaked on three dates in a row, or turned down three different forms of investment in a row, throw the ball in her court.

If you do it too early, you're likely not asking enough and/or not varying your requests enough to rule out her just not wanting to do some specific thing... rather than her out-and-out not wanting to go with you.

---

[47] GirlsChase.com – "A Devil May Care Attitude: What It Is & How to Get It"

In Summary...

The healthiest way to think about a parting shot ball's-in-your-court exit is this: you want to encourage her to follow up with you again (as much as possible). That's a big part of why that sweet spot of three different requests is so important.

If you do more than that, it feels like you're chasing, and you're not the kind of guy she wants to follow up with. Yet, if you do fewer than three, it doesn't feel like you're making a whole heck of a lot of effort to get her. Now if she follows up, she's going to feel like she is the one chasing. Most girls will shy away from this, even if they like you – they don't want to risk losing face.

What you're going for here in how you balance your ball's-in-your-court deals is for a girl to feel like you put out a valiant effort to make something happen with her... but stopped before crossing the line where it would turn into chasing. And then you walked away – but with an invitation for her to follow up with you again when she feels so inclined.

You balance the emotions here. You're not chasing, but you're also not investing so little that she feels like she's chasing if she contacts you again later.

Remember: **you must give a little**[48] if you want her to pursue.

Use this one right, and you'll avoid the two snags men get caught up in here: using the parting shot too much and too soon, or not using it at all. Hit that sweet spot in how and when you use it, and you'll turn go-nowhere scenarios into "she came back" ones.

---

[48] GirlsChase.com – "Get Girls Chasing: Give a Little to Get a Lot"

10

Example Text Conversation

While all this might seem complicated at first glance, the hard work's all at the start. What good texting leads to is vastly simpler text chats that line up dates like dominos. All said and done, here's an example text conversation, start to finish, to give you a feel for what this looks like:

[an hour after meeting a new girl]

You: Happy to have made your acquaintance, friend ;) - [your name]

[two hours later]

Her: Great to meet you too! :)

[36 hours later]

You: Hey Sandy, how'd the weekend turn out? Hope the rest of it was as awesome as the beginnings were :) I ended up going to a pizza party with a bunch of people Sunday night... Haven't been to one of those since I was 12. It was fun, though. And, some great pizza. On our bite this week - when's good for you? My schedule's pretty open except Tuesday and Wednesday nights. Let me know what day's best and we'll schedule it up.

[40 minutes later]

Her: Hey! The pizza party sounds amazing! My weekend was pretty chill... Mostly just recovering from Friday, lol. How's Thursday for meeting up? I'm free most of the day.

[25 minutes later]

You: Thursday's perfect. Say 1 o'clock in the afternoon? There's this amazing little café no one knows about on Green Avenue we can check out... They have the most mind-blowing crepes in the world. We can meet at the Green Ave subway stop, it's a short walk from there.

[1 hour later]

Her: That sounds great, let's do it! See you on Thursday!

[2 hours later]

You: Awesome - see you then, Sandy!

[Thursday, 12:30 PM]

You: Heading out the door in a few minutes, should be there right at 1 o'clock. I'll be at Exit 2C. See you soon!

[5 minutes later]

Her: Hey, I'm running about 10 minutes behind. Sorry...! I'm coming!

[3 minutes later]

You: No biggie. See you when you get here!

Now compare that to the last 10 texting conversations you had with women... which are more complicated, and which are less? The only complicated part here is in learning the process. Once you've got it down, you can execute it perfectly, efficiently, and consistently... and it's a thing of pure beauty.

And you'll sit there and look at the cell phones of those poor girls you're sleeping with or dating... and you'll see the volumes and volumes of clueless boring questions they get... endless conversations they're mired in... and really, incredibly witty and interesting texts they're inundated with... and you'll shake your head at the guys sending them.

"I used to be one of those guys," you'll say to yourself. "But *that*... was another *life*."

And then that thought will pass, and you'll probably never spend a second thought on texting again.

11

Where the Learning Curve Lies

Here are the biggest growth areas you can expect, depending on where you're at with texting.

Growth Areas for Beginner Texters

As a beginner, you'll want to focus most of your attention on the following areas:

Getting down timing. How fast or how slow should you respond? What days and at what times of day should you text? What kind of message do you send, and when?

Getting down structure. Your challenge will not just be to get used to using the proper text structure, but to stick to it. You'll likely feel tempted to "wing it." This temptation almost always leads you astray... especially when you're a beginner. Stick to best practices (what we covered in this book) and only experiment with new angles on girls you don't mind losing.

Anxiety over pulling the trigger. Sooner or later, you have to ask her out. Better to learn to do it sooner.

Growth Areas for Intermediate Texters

The most important areas to focus on as an intermediate texter are:

Getting down concision. As a beginner, you learned structure. Now it's time to be briefer. The more concise you can make your texts (while still cramming in everything you must cram in), the better. People respond best to messages that are short.

Interesting without being the fool. You want to include fun, humor, and interesting bits in your texts. However, you don't want to be the clownish entertainer. How you strike the right balance – where you aren't boring, but also not over the top – is one of your key challenges at this stage.

Engaging girls properly. How do you get girls to actually engage with you over text? How do you get them to take part? This is one of your biggest foci at this stage. As she participates more, she does more of the work to set things up, and makes the courtship more fun for you.

Arranging dates more smoothly. Here you'll target aspects like when and how you schedule dates, where you take girls on dates, and how you manage the convenience of dates. The better you get at this, the more yeses you'll get, and the fewer flakes you'll see.

Growth Areas for Advanced Texters

The primary targets for the advanced texter to improve upon are:

Cutting down texting even more. What's the bare minimum of texts you need to send before you can get a girl on a date? The closer to this you get, the less chance you give yourself to mess things up, and the sooner you'll get her out.

Getting girls to chase you and pursue you. Wouldn't it be nice if girls worked to set up dates themselves? This is something you'll find yourself playing with more at this stage (and starting to succeed at).

Getting very dominant and direct, both in how you set up your dates, and in how you handle the finer points of language structure in texts. The aim is to be powerfully dominant without being domineering. Attractive, rather than repulsive.

Working on assuming the sale. You'll be sending texts that just assume she's sold. "Shall we grab lunch? I'm thinking we could do O'Malley's at noon tomorrow; sound good?" The better you are at assuming the sale, the more you offload mental labor from her, and the easier it is for her to just say "yes."

Conclusion

Farewell for Now

There's a great deal of nuance in texting. But in the end, it's about simplicity. The simpler your texts are, the better a response they get. Of course, there's finesse to keeping things simple yet effective. That's why you bought this book!

If you read from cover to cover without picking up your phone, I hope you'll pick it up now. Try out the material from this book. Whether it's a first text to a new girl who's number you just got, or a check-in text with a girl you haven't talked to in a while, take this book for a spin. Try it with a number of different girls – at least 5 to 10 phone numbers. I think the night-and-day difference in responses you get will surprise you (in a great way).

Before we go, I have two free gifts to offer you for completing this book.

The first free gift is an audio podcast I put together exclusively for buyers of this book. I polled the Girls Chase audience and asked: "What is your BIGGEST unanswered question about texting girls?" I then took 79 of those questions and answered them in a 93-minute podcast.

Once you've finished this book and reviewed it from the store you purchased it at, please fill out the form on this page:

http://www.girlschase.com/bonus/how-to-text-book

All I need is your email address for me to send the podcast to. The podcast is 93 minutes long. I had a lot of fun recording it for you, and it covers these great questions:

1. How long should I spend in chit-chat, small talk, or flirting before I ask her out and take her phone number?
2. How do I capture the attention of girls who are likely receiving a ton of messages every day?
3. What do you do if a girl doesn't ask you any questions?
4. How do I start building tension fast?
5. If you're too busy to meet for a date right now, how do you keep her in the queue?
6. Is it better to talk less, or more?
7. How often should I be texting girls on average?
8. What do I do if she's slow at texting back?
9. Should you text every day? What do you do if the girl herself texts every day?
10. Is it possible to text a girl straight over to your place?
11. What do you do when you propose a date and get an excuse instead of a yes?
12. What should I text after a good first date, and how long do I wait?
13. Should you text girlfriends and friends with benefits outside of setting up logistics, or not?
14. Why do girls stop texting out of the blue?

... Plus 65 more fantastic questions. I think you'll get a lot of value out of it.

The second free gift is my introductory 7-day "Do Awesome with Girls" course. This course is part video, part book, part free report, and you get fresh content each day for a week. I'll send it to you after I send you the podcast, and I think you'll be pretty happy with the content. Guys love this course. It makes a big difference in their dating lives, and it's steeped in scientific research, too.

To get both free gifts, please visit the following link and provide me with your information:

http://www.girlschase.com/bonus/how-to-text-book

... And I'll get you those gifts in a jiffy.

I hope we talk again soon.

— **Chase Amante**

Appendix A
References

ANI. (2010). Text message fast becoming acceptable way of asking girl out down under. *The Hindustan Times*.

Critchley, H. D., Rotshtein, P., Nagai, Y., O'Doherty, J., Mathias, C. J., & Dolan, R. J. (2005). Activity in the human brain predicting differential heart rate responses to emotional facial expressions. *Neuroimage*, 24(3), 751-762.

Gunraj, D. N., Drumm-Hewitt, A. M., Dashow, E. M., Upadhyay, S. S. N., & Klin, C. M. (2016). Texting insincerely: The role of the period in text messaging. *Computers in Human Behavior*, 55, 1067-1075.

Holtgraves, T., & Paul, K. (2013). Texting versus talking: An exploration in telecommunication language. *Telematics and Informatics*, 30(4), 289-295.

Kock, N. (2004). The psychobiological model: Towards a new theory of computer-mediated communication based on Darwinian evolution. *Organization Science*, 15(3), 327-348.

Kock, N. (2005). Media richness or media naturalness? The evolution of our biological communication apparatus and its influence on our behavior toward e-communication tools. *IEEE Transactions on Professional Communication*, 48(2), 117-130.

Kock, N. (2007). Media naturalness and compensatory encoding: The burden of electronic media obstacles is on senders. *Decision Support Systems*, 44(1), 175-187.

LaBowe, C. J. (2011). Texting Versus Talking: Age Sex and Extroversion as Predictors of Frequency and Preference Among an Undergraduate Cohort.

Luo, S. (2014). Effects of texting on satisfaction in romantic relationships: The role of attachment. *Computers in Human Behavior, 33*, 145-152.

McLuhan, M. (1994). *Understanding media: The extensions of man*. MIT press.

Meenagh, J. (2015). Flirting, dating, and breaking up within new media environments. *Sex Education, 15*(5), 458-471.

Nakajima, T. (2014). Verifying the Foot-in-the-Mouth effect in printed materials. *Japanese Journal of Persuasion & Negotiation, 6*.

Ogletree, S. M., Fancher, J., & Gill, S. (2014). Gender and texting: Masculinity, femininity, and gender role ideology. *Computers in Human Behavior, 37*, 49-55.

Reid, D. J., & Reid, F. J. (2007). Text or talk? Social anxiety, loneliness, and divergent preferences for cell phone use. *CyberPsychology & Behavior, 10*(3), 424-435.

Reid, D. J., & Reid, F. J. M. (2004). The social and psychological effects of text messaging. *Journal of the British Computer Society*.

Rettie, R. (2007). Texters not talkers: phone aversion among mobile phone users. *PsychNology Journal, 5*(1), 33-57.

Skovholt, K., Grønning, A., & Kankaanranta, A. (2014). The Communicative Functions of Emoticons in Workplace E-Mails::-). *Journal of Computer-Mediated Communication, 19*(4), 780-797.

Vlahovic, T. A., Roberts, S., & Dunbar, R. (2012). Effects of duration and laughter on subjective happiness within different modes of communication. *Journal of Computer-Mediated Communication, 17*(4), 436-450.

Appendix B
GirlsChase.com Article URLs

Why Girls Like Bad Boys
http://www.girlschase.com/content/why-girls-bad-boys/

Why Nice Guys Finish Last
http://www.girlschase.com/content/why-nice-guys-finish-last/

Does She Want You as a Boyfriend... or Something Else?
http://www.girlschase.com/content/does-she-want-you-boyfriend-or-something-else/

How Victim Mentality Can Stifle Your Life – and Luck with Women
http://www.girlschase.com/content/how-victim-mentality-can-stifle-your-life-%E2%80%93-and-luck-women/

Get to Know a Girl: Connection-Building Tactics
http://www.girlschase.com/content/get-to-know-a-girl/

Just Friends: A Man's Worst Nightmare
http://www.girlschase.com/content/just-friends-mans-worst-nightmare/

How to Get Out of the Friend Zone: A Man's Survival Guide
http://www.girlschase.com/content/how-get-out-friend-zone-mans-survival-guide/

Dating and Relationship Precedent: Why It's So Very Important
http://www.girlschase.com/content/dating-and-relationship-precedent-why-it%E2%80%99s-so-very-important/

Date Templates: Minimize Confusion, Maximize Returns
http://www.girlschase.com/content/date-templates-minimize-confusion-maximize-returns/

Simplify Your Dates
http://www.girlschase.com/content/simplify-your-dates/

How to Break the Ice: 5 Surefire Ways to Entice Her
http://www.girlschase.com/content/how-break-ice-5-surefire-ways-entice-her/

The Law of Least Effort
http://www.girlschase.com/content/law-least-effort/

Secrets to Getting Girls: Staying Out of Auto-Rejection
http://www.girlschase.com/content/secrets-getting-girls-staying-out-auto-rejection/

Secrets to Getting Girls: Move Faster
http://www.girlschase.com/content/secrets-getting-girls-move-faster/

Sprezzatura, Effort, and Investing
http://www.girlschase.com/content/sprezzatura-effort-and-investing/

Are You Trying Too Hard? Stop Trying. Start Succeeding
http://www.girlschase.com/content/are-you-trying-too-hard-stop-trying-start-succeeding/

Secrets to Getting Girls: The Art of the Deep Dive
http://www.girlschase.com/content/secrets-getting-girls-art-deep-dive/

Nonverbal Communication
http://www.girlschase.com/content/nonverbal-communication/

The Real Reason Many Men Can't Get a Girl
http://www.girlschase.com/content/real-reason-many-men-cant-get-girl/

The Sad Tale of "Shopping Guy"
http://www.girlschase.com/content/sad-tale-shopping-guy/

The Party Date: Don't Do It
http://www.girlschase.com/content/party-date-dont-do-it/

Sexual Tension: 7 Ways to Make Women Excited and Randy
http://www.girlschase.com/content/sexual-tension-7-ways-make-women-excited-and-randy/

Secrets to Getting Girls: Natural Number Swapping
http://www.girlschase.com/content/secrets-getting-girls-natural-number-swapping/

How Girls Show Interest
http://www.girlschase.com/content/how-girls-show-interest/

Reactions from Women, or Results with Women?
http://www.girlschase.com/content/reactions-women-or-results-women/

Simplify Your Dates
http://www.girlschase.com/content/simplify-your-dates/

Fractionation Simply Explained
http://www.girlschase.com/content/fractionation-simply-explained/

A Good First Impression: Making One Every Time
http://www.girlschase.com/content/good-first-impression-making-one-every-time/

How to Get a Phone Number from a Girl Every Time You Ask
http://www.girlschase.com/content/how-get-phone-number-girl-every-time-you-ask/

How to Use Anchoring to Mesmerize Women
http://www.girlschase.com/content/how-use-anchoring-mesmerize-women/

Why Cold Approach Works Better Than Anything Else
http://www.girlschase.com/content/why-cold-approach-works-better-anything-else/

Do You Really Need to Learn Game to Get Girls?
http://www.girlschase.com/content/do-you-really-need-learn-game-get-girls/

Just Be Yourself: The Worst Dating Advice Known to Man
http://www.girlschase.com/content/just-be-yourself-worst-dating-advice-known-man/

How to Be an Asshole – and Become Adored by Women
http://www.girlschase.com/content/how-be-asshole-%E2%80%93-and-become-adored-women/

How Preselection Works to Get You Girls
http://www.girlschase.com/content/how-preselection-can-get-you-girls/

A Devil May Care Attitude: What It Is & How to Get It
http://www.girlschase.com/content/devil-may-care-attitude-what-it-how-get-it

Get Girls Chasing: Give a Little to Get a Lot
http://www.girlschase.com/content/get-girls-chasing-give-little-get-lot/

Made in the USA
Lexington, KY
09 January 2019